NOAM CHOMSKY

OPEN MEDIA COLLECTION

9-11
MEDIA CONTROL
ACTS OF AGGRESSION

NOAM CHOMSKY

OPEN MEDIA COLLECTION

9-11
MEDIA CONTROL
ACTS OF AGGRESSION

QUALITY PAPERBACK BOOK CLUB
NEW YORK

9-11

NOAM CHOMSKY

I would like to thank David Peterson and Shifra Stern for invaluable assistance with current media research particularly.
—NOAM CHOMSKY

CONTENTS

EDITOR'S NOTE

What follows is a set of interviews conducted with Noam Chomsky by a variety of interviewers during the first month following the attacks of September 11, 2001 on the World Trade Center and the Pentagon. The interviews were conducted largely via email, many with foreign journalists who speak and write English as a second language. Although some interviews were conducted as early as eight days after the attacks, edits, additions, and revisions consistent with the latest news continued up until the book left for the printer on October 15. As a result, interviews dated September may contain references to October events. Furthermore, in the process of editing, sections were cut in which questions or answers were repeated between interviews. However, occasionally a repeated fact or point has been intentionally left in, for emphasis.

As Chomsky wrote me during the editing process, "These facts have been completely removed from history. One has to practically scream them from the rooftops."

Greg Ruggiero
New York City

1.

NOT SINCE THE WAR OF 1812

Based on an interview with *Il Manifesto* (Italy),
September 19, 2001.

*Q: The fall of the Berlin Wall didn't claim any victims, but
it did profoundly change the geopolitical scene. Do you
think that the attacks of 9-11 could have a similar effect?*

CHOMSKY: The fall of the Berlin Wall was an event of great
importance and did change the geopolitical scene, but not in
the ways usually assumed, in my opinion. I've tried to
explain my reasons elsewhere and won't go into it now.

The horrifying atrocities of September 11 are something
quite new in world affairs, not in their scale and character,
but in the target. For the United States, this is the first time
since the War of 1812 that the national territory has been
under attack, or even threatened. Many commentators have
brought up a Pearl Harbor analogy, but that is misleading.
On December 7, 1941, military bases in two U.S. colonies

were attacked—not the national territory, which was never threatened. The U.S. preferred to call Hawaii a "territory," but it was in effect a colony. During the past several hundred years the U.S. annihilated the indigenous population (millions of people), conquered half of Mexico (in fact, the territories of indigenous peoples, but that is another matter), intervened violently in the surrounding region, conquered Hawaii and the Philippines (killing hundreds of thousands of Filipinos), and, in the past half century particularly, extended its resort to force throughout much of the world. The number of victims is colossal. For the first time, the guns have been directed the other way. That is a dramatic change.

The same is true, even more dramatically, of Europe. Europe has suffered murderous destruction, but from internal wars. Meanwhile European powers conquered much of the world with extreme brutality. With the rarest of exceptions, they were not under attack by their foreign victims. England was not attacked by India, nor Belgium by the Congo, nor Italy by Ethiopia, nor France by Algeria (also not regarded by France as "a colony"). It is not surprising, therefore, that Europe should be utterly shocked by the terrorist crimes of September 11. Again, not because of the scale, regrettably.

Exactly what this portends, no one can guess. But that it is something strikingly new is quite clear.

My impression is that these attacks won't offer us new political scenery, but that they rather confirm the existence

NOAM CHOMSKY

of a problem inside the "Empire." The problem concerns political authority and power. What do you think?

The likely perpetrators are a category of their own, but uncontroversially, they draw support from a reservoir of bitterness and anger over U.S. policies in the region, extending those of earlier European masters. There certainly is an issue of "political authority and power." In the wake of the attacks, the *Wall Street Journal* surveyed opinions of "moneyed Muslims" in the region: bankers, professionals, businessmen with ties to the United States. They expressed dismay and anger about U.S. support for harsh authoritarian states and the barriers that Washington places against independent development and political democracy by its policies of "propping up oppressive regimes." Their primary concern, however, was different: Washington's policies towards Iraq and towards Israel's military occupation. Among the great mass of poor and suffering people, similar sentiments are much more bitter, and they are also hardly pleased to see the wealth of the region flow to the West and to small Western-oriented elites and corrupt and brutal rulers backed by Western power. So there definitely are problems of authority and power. The immediately announced U.S. reaction was to deal with these problems by intensifying them. That is, of course, not inevitable. A good deal depends on the outcome of such considerations.

Is America having trouble governing the process of global-

ization—and I don't mean just in terms of national security or intelligence systems?

The U.S. doesn't govern the corporate globalization project, though it of course has a primary role. These programs have been arousing enormous opposition, primarily in the South, where mass protests could often be suppressed or ignored. In the past few years, the protests reached the rich countries as well, and hence became the focus of great concern to the powerful, who now feel themselves on the defensive, not without reason. There are very substantial reasons for the worldwide opposition to the particular form of investor-rights "globalization" that is being imposed, but this is not the place to go into that.

"Intelligent bombs" in Iraq, "humanitarian intervention" in Kosovo. The U.S.A. never used the word "war" to describe that. Now they are talking about war against a nameless enemy. Why?

At first the U.S. used the word "crusade," but it was quickly pointed out that if they hope to enlist their allies in the Islamic world, it would be a serious mistake, for obvious reasons. The rhetoric therefore shifted to "war." The Gulf War of 1991 was called a "war." The bombing of Serbia was called a "humanitarian intervention," by no means a novel usage. That was a standard description of European imperialist ventures in the 19th century. To cite some more recent

NOAM CHOMSKY

examples, the major recent scholarly work on "humanitarian intervention" cites three examples of "humanitarian intervention" in the immediate pre-World War II period: Japan's invasion of Manchuria, Mussolini's invasion of Ethiopia, and Hitler's takeover of the Sudetenland. The author of course is not suggesting that the term is apt; rather, that the crimes were masked as "humanitarian."

Whether the Kosovo intervention indeed was "humanitarian," possibly the first such case in history, is a matter of fact: passionate declaration does not suffice, if only because virtually every use of force is justified in these terms. It is quite extraordinary how weak the arguments are to justify the claim of humanitarian intent in the Kosovo case; more accurately, they scarcely exist, and the official government reasons are quite different. But that's a separate matter, which I've written about in some detail elsewhere.

But even the pretext of "humanitarian intervention" cannot be used in the normal way in the present case. So we are left with "war."

The proper term would be "crime"—perhaps "crime against humanity," as Robert Fisk has stressed. But there are laws for punishing crimes: identify the perpetrators, and hold them accountable, the course that is widely recommended in the Middle East, by the Vatican, and many others. But that requires solid evidence, and it opens doors to dangerous questions: to mention only the most obvious one, who were the perpetrators of the crime of international terrorism condemned by the World Court 15 years ago?

For such reasons, it is better to use a vague term, like "war." To call it a "war against terrorism," however, is simply more propaganda, unless the "war" really does target terrorism. But that is plainly not contemplated because Western powers could never abide by their own official definitions of the term, as in the U.S. Code* or Army manuals. To do so would at once reveal that the U.S. is a leading terrorist state, as are its clients.

Perhaps I may quote political scientist Michael Stohl: "We must recognize that by convention—and it must be emphasized only by convention—great power use and the threat of the use of force is normally described as coercive diplomacy and not as a form of terrorism," though it commonly involves "the threat and often the use of violence for what would be described as terroristic purposes were it not great powers who were pursuing the very same tactic," in accord with the literal meaning of the term. Under the (admittedly unimaginable) circumstances that Western intellectual culture were willing to adopt the literal meaning, the war against terrorism would take quite a different

---

* "[An] act of terrorism, means any activity that (A) involves a violent act or an act dangerous to human life that is a violation of the criminal laws of the United States or any State, or that would be a criminal violation if committed within the jurisdiction of the United States or of any State; and (B) appears to be intended (i) to intimidate or coerce a civilian population; (ii) to influence the policy of a government by intimidation or coercion; or (iii) to affect the conduct of a government by assassination or kidnapping." (United States Code Congressional and Administrative News, 98th Congress, Second Session, 1984, Oct. 19, volume 2; par. 3077, 98 STAT. 2707 [West Publishing Co., 1984]).

NOAM CHOMSKY

form, along lines spelled out in extensive detail in literature that does not enter the respectable canon.

The quote I just gave is cited in a survey volume called *Western State Terrorism*, edited by Alex George and published by a major publisher 10 years ago, but unmentionable in the United States. Stohl's point is then illustrated in detail throughout the book. And there are many others, extensively documented from the most reliable sources—for example, official government documents—but also unmentionable in the U.S., though the taboo is not so strict in other English-speaking countries, or elsewhere.

NATO is keeping quiet until they find out whether the attack was internal or external. How do you interpret this?

I do not think that that is the reason for NATO's hesitation. There is no serious doubt that the attack was "external." I presume that NATO's reasons for hesitation are those that European leaders are expressing quite publicly.

They recognize, as does everyone with close knowledge of the region, that a massive assault on a Muslim population would be the answer to the prayers of bin Laden and his associates, and would lead the U.S. and its allies into a "diabolical trap," as the French foreign minister put it.

Could you say something about connivance and the role of American secret service?

I don't quite understand the question. This attack was surely an enormous shock and surprise to the intelligence services of the West, including those of the United States. The CIA did have a role, a major one in fact, but that was in the 1980s, when it joined Pakistani intelligence and others (Saudi Arabia, Britain, etc.) in recruiting, training, and arming the most extreme Islamic fundamentalists it could find to fight a "Holy War" against the Russian invaders of Afghanistan.

The best source on this topic is the book *Unholy Wars*, written by longtime Middle East correspondent and author John Cooley. There is now, predictably, an effort under way to clean up the record and pretend that the U.S. was an innocent bystander, and a bit surprisingly, even respectable journals (not to speak of others) are soberly quoting CIA officials to "demonstrate" that required conclusion—in gross violation of the most elementary journalistic standards.

After that war was over, the "Afghanis" (many, like bin Laden, not Afghans), turned their attention elsewhere: for example, to Chechnya and Bosnia, where they may have received at least tacit U.S. support. Not surprisingly, they were welcomed by the governments; in Bosnia, many Islamic volunteers were granted citizenship in gratitude for their military services (Carlotta Gall, *New York Times*, October 2, 2001).

And to western China, where they are fighting for liberation from Chinese domination; these are Chinese Muslims, some apparently sent by China to Afghanistan as early as

1978 to join a guerrilla rebellion against the government, later joining the CIA-organized forces after the Russian invasion in 1979 in support of the government Russia backed—and installed, much as the U.S. installed a government in South Vietnam and then invaded to "defend" the country it was attacking, to cite a fairly close analog. And in the southern Philippines, North Africa, and elsewhere, fighting for the same causes, as they see it. They also turned their attention to their prime enemies Saudi Arabia, Egypt, and other Arab states, and by the 1990s, also to the U.S. (which bin Laden regards as having invaded Saudi Arabia much as Russia invaded Afghanistan).

What consequences do you foresee for the Seattle movement? Do you think it will suffer as a result, or is it possible that it will gain momentum?

It is certainly a setback for the worldwide protests against corporate globalization, which—again—did not begin in Seattle. Such terrorist atrocities are a gift to the harshest and most repressive elements on all sides, and are sure to be exploited—already have been in fact—to accelerate the agenda of militarization, regimentation, reversal of social democratic programs, transfer of wealth to narrow sectors, and undermining democracy in any meaningful form. But that will not happen without resistance, and I doubt that it will succeed, except in the short term.

What are the consequences for the Middle East? In particular for the Israeli-Palestinian conflict?

The atrocities of September 11 were a devastating blow for the Palestinians, as they instantly recognized. Israel is openly exulting in the "window of opportunity" it now has to crush Palestinians with impunity. In the first few days after the 9-11 attack, Israeli tanks entered Palestinian cities (Jenin, Ramallah, Jericho for the first time), several dozen Palestinians were killed, and Israel's iron grip on the population tightened, exactly as would be expected. Again, these are the common dynamics of a cycle of escalating violence, familiar throughout the world: Northern Ireland, Israel-Palestine, the Balkans, and elsewhere.

How do you judge the reaction of Americans? They seemed pretty cool-headed, but as Saskia Sassen recently said in an interview, "We already feel as though we are at war."

The immediate reaction was shock, horror, anger, fear, a desire for revenge. But public opinion is mixed, and countercurrents did not take long to develop. They are now even being recognized in mainstream commentary. Today's newspapers, for example.

In an interview you gave to the Mexican daily La Jornada, *you said that we are faced with a new type of war. What exactly did you mean?*

It is a new type of war for the reasons mentioned in response to your first question: the guns are now aimed in a different direction, something quite new in the history of Europe and its offshoots.

Are Arabs, by definition, necessarily fundamentalist, the West's new enemy?

Certainly not. First of all, no one with even a shred of rationality defines Arabs as "fundamentalist." Secondly, the U.S. and the West generally have no objection to religious fundamentalism as such. The U.S., in fact, is one of the most extreme religious fundamentalist cultures in the world; not the state, but the popular culture. In the Islamic world, the most extreme fundamentalist state, apart from the Taliban, is Saudi Arabia, a U.S. client state since its origins; the Taliban are in fact an offshoot of the Saudi version of Islam.

Radical Islamist extremists, often called "fundamentalists," were U.S. favorites in the 1980s, because they were the best killers who could be found. In those years, a prime enemy of the U.S. was the Catholic Church, which had sinned grievously in Latin America by adopting "the preferential option for the poor," and suffered bitterly for that crime. The West is quite ecumenical in its choice of enemies. The criteria are subordination and service to power, not religion. There are many other illustrations.

2.

IS THE WAR ON TERRORISM WINNABLE?

Based on separate interviews with Kevin Canfield of the *Hartford Courant* on September 20, 2001, and David Barsamian on September 21, 2001.

Q: Is the nation's so-called war on terrorism winnable? If yes, how? If no, then what should the Bush administration do to prevent attacks like the ones that struck New York and Washington?

CHOMSKY: If we want to consider this question seriously, we should recognize that in much of the world the U.S. is regarded as a leading terrorist state, and with good reason. We might bear in mind, for example, that in 1986 the U.S. was condemned by the World Court for "unlawful use of force" (international terrorism) and then vetoed a Security Council resolution calling on all states (meaning the U.S.) to adhere to international law. Only one of countless examples.

But to keep to the narrow question—the terrorism of others directed against us—we know quite well how the problem should be addressed, if we want to reduce the threat rather than escalate it. When IRA bombs were set off in London, there was no call to bomb West Belfast, or Boston, the source of much of the financial support for the IRA. Rather, steps were taken to apprehend the criminals, and efforts were made to deal with what lay behind the resort to terror. When a federal building was blown up in Oklahoma City, there were calls for bombing the Middle East, and it probably would have happened if the source turned out to be there. When it was found to be domestic, with links to the ultra-right militias, there was no call to obliterate Montana and Idaho. Rather, there was a search for the perpetrator, who was found, brought to court, and sentenced, and there were efforts to understand the grievances that lie behind such crimes and to address the problems. Just about every crime—whether a robbery in the streets or colossal atrocities—has reasons, and commonly we find that some of them are serious and should be addressed.

There are proper and lawful ways to proceed in the case of crimes, whatever their scale. And there are precedents. A clear example is the one I just mentioned, one that should be entirely uncontroversial, because of the reaction of the highest international authorities.

Nicaragua in the 1980s was subjected to violent assault by the U.S. Tens of thousands of people died. The country was substantially destroyed; it may never recover. The international terrorist attack was accompanied by a devastating economic war, which a small country isolated by a vengeful and cruel superpower could scarcely sustain, as the leading historians of Nicaragua, Thomas Walker for one, have reviewed in detail. The effects on the country are much more severe even than the tragedies in New York the other day. They didn't respond by setting off bombs in Washington. They went to the World Court, which ruled in their favor, ordering the U.S. to desist and pay substantial reparations. The U.S. dismissed the court judgment with contempt, responding with an immediate escalation of the attack. So Nicaragua then went to the Security Council, which considered a resolution calling on states to observe international law. The U.S. alone vetoed it. They went to the General Assembly, where they got a similar resolution that passed with the U.S. and Israel opposed two years in a row (joined once by El Salvador). That's the way a state should proceed. If Nicaragua had been powerful enough, it could have set up another criminal court. Those are the measures the U.S. could pursue, and nobody's going to block it. That's what they're being asked to do by people throughout the region, including their allies.

Remember, the governments in the Middle East and North Africa, like the terrorist Algerian government, which is one of the most vicious of all, would be happy to join the U.S. in opposing terrorist networks which are attacking them. They're the prime targets. But they have been asking for some evidence, and they want to do it in a framework of at least minimal commitment to international law. The Egyptian position is complex. They're part of the primary system that organized the radical Islamic forces of which the bin Laden network was a part. They were the first victims of it when Sadat was assassinated. They've been major victims of it since. They'd like to crush it, but, they say, only after some evidence is presented about who's involved and within the framework of the UN Charter, under the aegis of the Security Council.

That is the course one follows if the intention is to reduce the probability of further atrocities. There is another course: react with extreme violence, and expect to escalate the cycle of violence, leading to still further atrocities such as the one that is inciting the call for revenge. The dynamic is very familiar.

What aspect or aspects of the story have been underreported by the mainstream press, and why is it important that they be paid more attention?

There are several fundamental questions:

First, what courses of action are open to us, and what are their likely consequences? There has been virtually no discussion of the option of adhering to the rule of law, as others do, for example Nicaragua, which I just mentioned (failing, of course, but no one will bar such moves by the U.S.) or as England did in the case of the IRA, or as the U.S. did when it was found that the Oklahoma City bombing was domestic in origin. And innumerable other cases.

Rather, there has, so far, been a solid drumbeat of calls for

NOAM CHOMSKY

violent reaction, with only scarce mention of the fact that this will not only visit a terrible cost on wholly innocent victims, many of them Afghan victims of the Taliban, but also that it will answer the most fervent prayers of bin Laden and his network.

The second question is: "why?" This question is rarely raised in any serious way.

To refuse to face this question is to choose to increase significantly the probability of further crimes of this kind. There have been some exceptions. As I mentioned earlier, the *Wall Street Journal*, to its credit, reviewed the opinions of "moneyed Muslims," people who are pro-American but severely critical of U.S. policies in the region, for reasons that are familiar to anyone who has paid any attention. The feelings in the streets are similar, though far more bitter and angry.

The bin Laden network itself falls into a different category, and in fact its actions for 20 years have caused great harm to the poor and oppressed people of the region, who are not the concern of the terrorist networks. But they do draw from a reservoir of anger, fear, and desperation, which is why they are praying for a violent U.S. reaction, which will mobilize others to their horrendous cause.

Such topics as these should occupy the front pages—at least, if we hope to reduce the cycle of violence rather than to escalate it.

3.

THE IDEOLOGICAL CAMPAIGN

Based on separate interviews with Radio B92 (Belgrade) on
September 18, 2001, Elise Fried and Peter Kreysler for
DeutschlandFunk Radio (Germany) on September 20, 2001,
and Paola Leoni for *Giornale del Popolo* (Switzerland)
on September 21, 2001.

*Q: How do you see the media coverage of this event? Is
there a parallel to the Gulf War in "manufacturing consent"?*

CHOMSKY: Media coverage is not quite as uniform as
Europeans seem to believe, perhaps because they are keeping
to the *New York Times*, National Public Radio, TV, and so
on. Even the *New York Times* conceded, this morning, that
attitudes in New York are quite unlike those they have been
conveying. It's a good story, also hinting at the fact that the
mainstream media have not been reporting this, which is
not entirely true, though it has been true, pretty much, of
the *New York Times*.

The *Times* now reports that "the drumbeat for war…is
barely audible on the streets of New York," and that calls for
peace "far outnumber demands for retribution," even at the

main "outdoor memorial to loss and grief" for the victims of the atrocity. In fact, that's not unusual around the country. There is surely virtually unanimous sentiment, which all of us share, for apprehending and punishing the perpetrators, if they can be found. But I think there is probably strong majority sentiment against lashing out blindly and killing plenty of innocent people.

But it is entirely typical for the major media, and the intellectual classes generally, to line up in support of power at a time of crisis and try to mobilize the population for the same cause. That was true, with almost hysterical intensity, at the time of the bombing of Serbia. The Gulf War was not at all unusual.

And the pattern goes far back in history.

Assuming that the terrorists chose the World Trade Center as a symbolic target, how does globalization and cultural hegemony help create hatred towards America?

This is an extremely convenient belief for Western intellectuals. It absolves them of responsibility for the actions that actually do lie behind the choice of the World Trade Center. Was it bombed in 1993 because of concern over globalization and cultural hegemony? Was Sadat assassinated 20 years ago because of globalization? Is that why the "Afghanis" of the CIA-backed forces fought Russia in Afghanistan, or in Chechnya now?

A few days ago the *Wall Street Journal* reported attitudes

of rich and privileged Egyptians who were at a McDonald's restaurant wearing stylish American clothes, etc., and who were bitterly critical of the U.S. for objective reasons of policy, which are well-known to those who wish to know: they had a report a few days earlier on attitudes of wealthy and privileged people in the region, all pro-American, and harshly critical of U.S. policies. Is that concern over "globalization," McDonald's, and jeans? Attitudes in the street are similar, but far more intense, and have nothing at all to do with these fashionable excuses.

These excuses are convenient for the U.S. and much of the West. To quote the lead analysis in the *New York Times* (September 16): "the perpetrators acted out of hatred for the values cherished in the West as freedom, tolerance, prosperity, religious pluralism and universal suffrage." U.S. actions are irrelevant, and therefore need not even be mentioned (Serge Schmemann). This is a comforting picture, and the general stance is not unfamiliar in intellectual history; in fact, it is close to the norm. It happens to be completely at variance with everything we know, but has all the merits of self-adulation and uncritical support for power. And it has the flaw that adopting it contributes significantly to the likelihood of further atrocities, including atrocities directed against us, perhaps even more horrendous ones than those of 9-11.

As for the bin Laden network, they have as little concern for globalization and cultural hegemony as they do for the poor and oppressed people of the Middle East who they have been severely harming for years. They tell us what their concerns are loud and clear: they are fighting a Holy War against the corrupt, repressive, and "un-Islamist" regimes of the region, and their supporters, just as they fought a Holy War against the Russians in the 1980s (and are now doing in Chechnya, western China, Egypt—in this case since 1981, when they assassinated Sadat—and elsewhere).

Bin Laden himself has probably never even heard of "globalization." Those who have interviewed him in depth, like Robert Fisk, report that he knows virtually nothing of the world and doesn't care to. We can choose to ignore all the facts and wallow in self-indulgent fantasies if we like, but at considerable risk to ourselves, among others. Among other things, we can also ignore, if we choose, the roots of the "Afghanis" such as bin Laden and his associates, also not a secret.

Are the American people educated to see this? Is there an awareness of cause and effect?

Unfortunately not, just as European people are not. What is crucially important to privileged elements in the Middle East region (and even more so on the streets) is scarcely understood here, particularly the most striking example: the contrasting U.S. policies toward Iraq and Israel's military occupation.

In Iraq, though Westerners prefer a different story, they see that U.S. policy in the past ten years has devastated the civilian society while strengthening Saddam Hussein—who, as they know, the U.S. strongly supported through his worst atrocities, including the gassing of the Kurds in 1988. When bin Laden makes these points in the broadcasts heard throughout the region, his audience understands, even those who despise him, as many do. About the U.S. and Israel, the most important facts are scarcely even reported and are almost universally unknown, to elite intellectuals in particular.

People of the region do not, of course, share the comforting illusions prevalent in the U.S. about the "generous" and "magnanimous" offers at Camp David in summer 2000, let alone other favored myths.

There is extensive material in print on this, well documented from uncontroversial sources, but it is scarcely known.

How do you see the reaction of the American government? Whose will are they representing?

The United States government, like others, primarily responds to centers of concentrated domestic power. That should be a truism. Of course, there are other influences, including popular currents—that is true of all societies, even brutal totalitarian systems, and surely more democratic ones. Insofar as we have information, the U.S. government is now trying to exploit the opportunity to ram through its own agenda: militarization, including "missile defense," code words for the militarization of space; undermining social democratic programs; also undermining concerns over the harsh effects of corporate "globalization," or environmental issues, or health insurance, and so on; instituting measures that will intensify the transfer of wealth to the very few (for example, eliminating corporate taxes); and regimenting the society, so as to eliminate public debate and protest. All normal, and entirely natural. As for a response, they are, I presume, listening to foreign leaders, specialists on the Middle East, and I suppose their own intelligence agencies, who are warning them that a massive military response will answer bin Laden's prayers. But there are hawkish elements who want to use the occasion to strike out at their enemies, with extreme violence, no matter how many innocent people suffer, including people here and in Europe who will be victims of the escalating cycle of violence. All again in a very familiar dynamic. There are plenty of bin Ladens on both sides, as usual.

Economic globalization has spread the Western model all over the world, and the U.S.A. has been its prime supporter, sometimes with questionable means, often humiliating local cultures. Are we facing the consequences of the last decades of American strategic policy? Is America an innocent victim?

This thesis is commonly advanced. I don't agree. One reason is that the Western model—notably, the U.S. model—is based on vast state intervention into the economy. The "neoliberal rules" are like those of earlier eras. They are double-edged: market discipline is good for you, but not for me, except for temporary advantage, when I am in a good position to win the competition.

Secondly, what happened on September 11 has virtually nothing to do with economic globalization, in my opinion. The reasons lie elsewhere. Nothing can justify crimes such as those of September 11, but we can think of the United States as an "innocent victim" only if we adopt the convenient path of ignoring the record of its actions and those of its allies, which are, after all, hardly a secret.

Everybody agrees that nothing will be the same after 9-11, from a restriction of rights in daily life up to global strategy with new alliances and new enemies. What is your opinion about this?

[*Editor's note: Chomsky's response to this question, edited here, began by reiterating a point made in an earlier interview that September 11 was the first time since the War of 1812 that the national territory of the U.S. was attacked by foreign forces. See page 11.*]

I do not think it will lead to a long-term restriction of rights internally in any serious sense. The cultural and institutional barriers to that are too firmly rooted, I believe. If the U.S. chooses to respond by escalating the cycle of violence, which is most likely what bin Laden and his associates hope for, then the consequences could be awesome. There are, of course, other ways, lawful and constructive ones. And there are ample precedents for them. An aroused public within the more free and democratic societies can direct policies towards a much more humane and honorable course.

Worldwide intelligence services and the international systems of control (Echelon, for example) could not foresee what was going to happen, even if the international Islamic terrorism network was not unknown. How is it possible that the Big Brother's eyes were shut? Do we have to fear, now, a Bigger Big Brother?

I frankly have never been overly impressed with concerns widely voiced in Europe over Echelon as a system of control. As for worldwide intelligence systems, their failures over the years have been colossal, a matter I and others have written about and that I cannot pursue here.

That is true even when the targets of concern are far easier to deal with than the bin Laden network, which is no doubt so decentralized, so lacking in hierarchical structure, and so dispersed throughout much of the world as to have become largely impenetrable. The intelligence services will no doubt be given resources to try harder. But a serious effort to reduce the threat of this kind of terrorism, as in innumerable other cases, requires an effort to understand and to address the causes.

Bin Laden, the devil: is this an enemy or rather a brand, a sort of logo which identifies and personalizes the evil?

NOAM CHOMSKY

Bin Laden may or may not be directly implicated in these acts, but it is likely that the network in which he was a prime figure is—that is, the forces established by the United States and its allies for their own purposes and supported as long as they served those purposes. It is much easier to personalize the enemy, identified as the symbol of ultimate evil, than to seek to understand what lies behind major atrocities. And there are, naturally, very strong temptations to ignore one's own role—which in this case, is not difficult to unearth, and indeed is familiar to everyone who has any knowledge of the region and its recent history.

Doesn't this war risk becoming a new Vietnam? That trauma is still alive.

That is an analogy that is often raised. It reveals, in my opinion, the profound impact of several hundred years of imperial violence on the intellectual and moral culture of the West. The war in Vietnam began as a U.S. attack against South Vietnam, which was always the main target of the U.S. wars, and ended by devastating much of Indochina. Unless we are willing to face that elementary fact, we cannot talk seriously about the Vietnam war. It is true that the war proved costly to the U.S., though the impact on Indochina was incomparably more awful. The invasion of Afghanistan also proved costly to the U.S.S.R., but that is not the problem that comes to the fore when we consider that crime.

4.

CRIMES OF STATE

Based on excerpts from an interview with
David Barsamian on September 21, 2001.

Q: As you know, there is rage, anger and bewilderment in the U.S. since the September 11 events. There have been murders, attacks on mosques and even a Sikh temple. The University of Colorado, which is located here in Boulder, a town which has a liberal reputation, has graffiti saying, "Go home, Arabs," "Bomb Afghanistan," and "Go Home, Sand Niggers." What's your perspective on what has evolved since the terrorist attacks?

CHOMSKY: It's mixed. What you're describing certainly exists. On the other hand, countercurrents exist. I know they do where I have direct contacts, and hear the same from others.

[Editor's note: Chomsky's response, edited here, echoes a comment he made in a previous interview in which he

describes the mood in New York City and the emergence of a peace movement. See page 29.]

That's another kind of current, also supportive of people who are being targeted here because they look dark or have a funny name. So there are countercurrents. The question is, what can we do to make the right ones prevail?

Do you think it's more than problematic to engage in alliances with individuals who are called "unsavory characters," drug traffickers and assassins, in order to achieve what is said to be a noble end?

Remember that some of the most unsavory characters are in the governments of the region, as well as in our own government, and the governments of our allies. If we're serious about it, we also have to ask, What is a noble end? Was it a noble end to draw the Russians into an "Afghan trap" in 1979, as Zbigniew Brzezinski claims he did? Supporting resistance against the Russian invasion in December 1979 is one thing. But inciting the invasion, as Brzezinski claims proudly that he did, and organizing a terrorist army of Islamic fanatics for your own purposes, is a different thing.

Another question we should be asking now is, What about the alliance that's being formed, that the U.S. is trying to put together? We should not forget that the U.S. itself is a leading terrorist state. What about the alliance between the U.S., Russia, China, Indonesia, Egypt, Algeria, all of whom are delighted to see an international system develop sponsored by the U.S. which will authorize them to carry out their own terrorist atrocities? Russia, for example, would be very happy to have U.S. backing for its murderous war in Chechnya. You have the same Afghanis fighting against Russia, also probably carrying out terrorist acts within Russia. As would perhaps India, in Kashmir. Indonesia would be delighted to have support for its massacres in Aceh. Algeria, as just announced on the broadcast we heard, would be delighted to have authorization to extend its own state terrorism. [*Editor's note: The broadcast Chomsky is referring to was the news report that aired immediately before his and Barsamian's live interview on KGNU (Boulder, Colorado).*] The same with China, fighting against separatist forces in its western provinces, including "Afghanis" who China and Iran had organized to fight the war against the Russians, beginning maybe as early as 1978, some reports indicate. And that runs through the world.

Not everyone will be admitted so easily into the coalition, however: we must, after all, maintain some standards. "The Bush administration warned [on October 6] that the leftist Sandinista party in Nicaragua, which hopes to return to power in elections next month, has maintained ties" with terrorist states and organizations, and therefore "cannot be counted on to support the international anti-terrorism coalition the administration has been attempting to forge" (George Gedda, AP, October 6). "As we stated previously there is no middle ground between those who oppose terrorism and those who support it," State Department spokeswoman Eliza Koch declared. Though the Sandinistas claim to have "abandoned the socialist policies and anti-American rhetoric of the past, Koch's statement [of October 6] indicated the administration has doubts about the claims of moderation." Washington's doubts are understandable. After all, Nicaragua had so outrageously attacked the U.S. that Ronald Reagan was compelled to declare a "national emergency" on May 1, 1985, renewed annually, because "the policies and actions of the Government of Nicaragua constitute an unusual and extraordinary threat to the national security and foreign policy of the United States." He also announced an embargo against Nicaragua "in response to the emergency situation created by the Nicaraguan Government's aggressive activities in Central America," namely its resistance to U.S. attack; the World Court dismissed as groundless Washington's claims of other activities. A year earlier, Reagan had designated May 1 as "Law Day," a celebration of our "200-year-old partnership between law and liberty," adding that without law there can be only "chaos and disorder." The day before, he celebrated Law Day by announcing that the United States would disregard the proceedings of the World Court, which went on to condemn his administration for its "unlawful use of force" and violation of treaties in its attack against Nicaragua, instantly escalated in response to the Court order to terminate the crime of international terrorism. Outside the U.S., of course, May 1 is a day of solidarity with the struggles of American workers.

It is, then, understandable that the U.S. should seek firm guarantees of good behavior before allowing a Sandinista-led Nicaragua to join the alliance of the just led by Washington, which is now welcoming others to join the war it has been waging against terrorism for 20 years: Russia, China, Indonesia, Turkey, and other worthy states, though of course not everyone.

Or, take the "Northern Alliance" that the U.S. and Russia are now jointly supporting. This is mostly a collection of warlords who carried out such destruction and terror that much of the population welcomed the Taliban. Furthermore, they are almost certainly involved in drug trafficking into Tajikistan. They control most of that border, and Tajikistan is reported to be a—maybe the—major transit point for the flow of drugs eventually to Europe and the United States. If the U.S. proceeds to join Russia in arming these forces heavily and launching some kind of offensive based on them, the drug flow is likely to increase under the ensuing conditions of chaos and refugee flight. The "unsavory characters" are, after all, familiar from a rich historical record, and the same is true of the "noble ends."

Your comment that the U.S. is a "leading terrorist state" might stun many Americans. Could you elaborate on that?

The most obvious example, though far from the most extreme case, is Nicaragua. It is the most obvious because it is uncontroversial, at least to people who have even the faintest concern for international law. [*Editor's note: See page 24 for Chomsky's more detailed elaboration on this point.*] It is worth remembering—particularly since it has been so uniformly suppressed—that the U.S. is the only country that was condemned for international terrorism by the World Court and that rejected a Security Council resolution calling on states to observe international law.

The United States continues international terrorism. There are also what in comparison are minor examples. Everybody here was quite properly outraged by the Oklahoma City bombing, and for a couple of days the headlines read, "Oklahoma City Looks Like Beirut." I didn't see anybody point out that Beirut also looks like Beirut, and part of the reason is that the Reagan administration had set off a terrorist bombing there in 1985 that was very much like Oklahoma City, a truck bombing outside a mosque timed to kill the maximum number of people as they left. It killed 80 and wounded 250, mostly women and children, according to a report in the *Washington Post* 3 years later. The terrorist bombing was aimed at a Muslim cleric whom they didn't like and whom they missed. It was not very secret. I don't know what name you give to the policies that are a leading factor in the death of maybe a million civilians in Iraq and maybe a half a million children, which is the price the Secretary of State says we're willing to pay. Is there a name for that? Supporting Israeli atrocities is another one.

Supporting Turkey's crushing of its own Kurdish population, for which the Clinton administration gave the decisive support, 80 percent of the arms, escalating as atrocities increased, is another. And that was a truly massive atrocity, one of the worst campaigns of ethnic cleansing and destruction in the 1990s, scarcely known because of the primary U.S. responsibility—and when impolitely brought up, dismissed as a minor "flaw" in our general dedication to "ending inhumanity" everywhere.

Or take the destruction of the Al-Shifa pharmaceutical plant in Sudan, one little footnote in the record of state terror, quickly forgotten. What would the reaction have been if the bin Laden network had blown up half the pharmaceutical supplies in the U.S. and the facilities for replenishing them? We can imagine, though the comparison is unfair: the consequences are vastly more severe in Sudan. That aside, if the U.S. or Israel or England were to be the target of such an atrocity, what would the reaction be? In this case we say, "Oh, well, too bad, minor mistake, let's go on to the next topic, let the victims rot." Other people in the world don't react like that. When bin Laden brings up that bombing, he strikes a resonant chord, even among those who despise and fear him; and the same, unfortunately, is true of much of the rest of his rhetoric.

Though it is merely a footnote, the Sudan case is nonetheless highly instructive. One interesting aspect is the reaction when someone dares to mention it. I have in the past, and did so again in response to queries from journalists shortly after the 9-11 atrocities. I mentioned that the toll of the "horrendous crime" of 9-11, committed with "wickedness and awesome cruelty" (quoting Robert Fisk), may be comparable to the consequences of Clinton's bombing of the Al-Shifa plant in August 1998. That plausible conclusion elicited an extraordinary reaction, filling many web sites and journals with feverish and fanciful condemnations, which I'll ignore. The only important aspect is that that single sentence—which, on a closer look, appears to be an understatement—was regarded by some commentators as utterly scandalous. It is difficult to avoid the conclusion that at some deep level, however they may deny it to themselves, they regard our crimes against the weak to be as normal as the air we breathe. Our crimes, for which we are responsible: as taxpayers, for failing to provide massive reparations, for granting refuge and immunity to the perpetrators, and for allowing the terrible facts to be sunk deep in the memory hole. All of this is of great significance, as it has been in the past.

About the consequences of the destruction of the Al-Shifa plant, we have only estimates. Sudan sought a UN inquiry into the justifications for the bombing, but even that was blocked by Washington, and few seem to have tried to investigate beyond. But we surely should. Perhaps we should begin by recalling some virtual truisms, at least among those with a minimal concern for human rights. When we estimate the human toll of a crime, we count not only those who were literally murdered on the spot but those who died as a result. That is the course we adopt reflexively, and properly, when we consider the crimes of official enemies—

Stalin, Hitler, and Mao, to mention the most extreme cases. Here, we do not consider the crime to be mitigated by the fact that it was not intended but was a reflection of institutional and ideological structures: the Chinese famine of 1958-1961, to take an extreme case, is not dismissed on grounds that it was a "mistake" and that Mao did not "intend" to kill tens of millions of people. Nor is it mitigated by speculations about his personal reasons for the orders that led to the famine. Similarly, we would dismiss with contempt the charge that condemnation of Hitler's crimes in Eastern Europe overlooks Stalin's crimes. If we are even pretending to be serious, we apply the same standards to ourselves, always. In this case, we count the number who died as a consequence of the crime, not just those killed in Khartoum by cruise missiles; and we do not consider the crime to be mitigated by the fact that it reflects the normal functioning of policymaking and ideological institutions— as it did, even if there is some validity to the (to my mind, dubious) speculations about Clinton's personal problems, which are irrelevant to this question anyway, for the reasons that everyone takes for granted when considering the crimes of official enemies.

With these truisms in mind, let's have a look at some of the material that was readily available in the mainstream press. I disregard the extensive analysis of the validity of Washington's pretexts, of little moral significance in comparison to the question of consequences.

A year after the attack, "without the lifesaving medicine

[the destroyed facilities] produced, Sudan's death toll from the bombing has continued, quietly, to rise... Thus, tens of thousands of people—many of them children—have suffered and died from malaria, tuberculosis, and other treatable diseases... [Al-Shifa] provided affordable medicine for humans and all the locally available veterinary medicine in Sudan. It produced 90 percent of Sudan's major pharmaceutical products... Sanctions against Sudan make it impossible to import adequate amounts of medicines required to cover the serious gap left by the plant's destruction... [T]he action taken by Washington on August 20, 1998, continues to deprive the people of Sudan of needed medicine. Millions must wonder how the International Court of Justice in The Hague will celebrate this anniversary" (Jonathan Belke, *Boston Globe*, August 22, 1999).

Germany's Ambassador to Sudan writes that "It is difficult to assess how many people in this poor African country died as a consequence of the destruction of the Al-Shifa factory, but several tens of thousands seems a reasonable guess" (Werner Daum, "Universalism and the West," *Harvard International Review*, Summer 2001).

"[T]he loss of this factory is a tragedy for the rural communities who need these medicines" (Tom Carnaffin, technical manager with "intimate knowledge" of the destroyed plant, quoted in Ed Vulliamy, Henry McDonald, Shyam Bhatia, and Martin Bright, *London Observer*, August 23, 1998, lead story, page 1).

Al-Shifa "provided 50 percent of Sudan's medicines, and its

NOAM CHOMSKY

destruction has left the country with no supplies of chloroquine, the standard treatment for malaria," but months later,
the British Labour government refused requests "to resupply
chloroquine in emergency relief until such time as the
Sudanese can rebuild their pharmaceutical production"
(Patrick Wintour, *Observer*, December 20, 1998).

The Al-Shifa facility was "the only one producing TB
drugs—for more than 100,000 patients, at about 1 British
pound a month. Costlier imported versions are not an option
for most of them—or for their husbands, wives and children,
who will have been infected since. Al-Shifa was also the
only factory making veterinary drugs in this vast, mostly
pastoralist, country. Its speciality was drugs to kill the para-
sites which pass from herds to herders, one of Sudan's principal causes of infant mortality" (James Astill, *Guardian*,
October 2, 2001).

The silent death toll continues to mount.

These accounts are by respected journalists writing in
leading journals. The one exception is the most knowledge-
able of the sources just cited, Jonathan Belke, regional program manager for the Near East Foundation, who writes on
the basis of field experience in Sudan. The Foundation is a
respected development institution dating back to World War
I. It provides technical assistance to poor countries in the
Middle East and Africa, emphasizing grassroots locally-run
development projects, and operates with close connections
to major universities, charitable organizations, and the State
Department, including well-known Middle East diplomats

and prominent figures in Middle East educational and developmental affairs.

According to credible analyses readily available to us, then, proportional to population, the destruction of Al-Shifa is as if the bin Laden network, in a single attack on the U.S., caused "hundreds of thousands of people—many of them children—to suffer and die from easily treatable diseases," though the analogy, as noted, is unfair. Sudan is "one of the least developed areas in the world. Its harsh climate, scattered populations, health hazards and crumbling infrastructure combine to make life for many Sudanese a struggle for survival"; a country with endemic malaria, tuberculosis, and many other diseases, where "periodic outbreaks of meningitis or cholera are not uncommon," so affordable medicines are a dire necessity (Jonathan Belke and Kamal El-Faki, technical reports from the field for the Near East Foundation). It is, furthermore, a country with limited arable land, a chronic shortage of potable water, a huge death rate, little industry, an unserviceable debt, wracked with AIDS, devastated by a vicious and destructive internal war, and under severe sanctions. What is happening within is largely speculation, including Belke's (quite plausible) estimate that within a year tens of thousands had already "suffered and died" as the result of the destruction of the major facilities for producing affordable drugs and veterinary medicines.

This only scratches the surface.

Human Rights Watch immediately reported that as an

immediate consequence of the bombing, "all UN agencies based in Khartoum have evacuated their American staff, as have many other relief organizations," so that "many relief efforts have been postponed indefinitely, including a crucial one run by the U.S.-based International Rescue Committee [in a government town] where more than fifty southerners are dying daily"; these are regions in "southern Sudan, where the UN estimates that 2.4 million people are at risk of starvation," and the "disruption in assistance" for the "devastated population" may produce a "terrible crisis."

What is more, the U.S. bombing "appears to have shattered the slowly evolving move toward compromise between Sudan's warring sides" and terminated promising steps towards a peace agreement to end the civil war that had left 1.5 million dead since 1981, which might have also led to "peace in Uganda and the entire Nile Basin." The attack apparently "shattered...the expected benefits of a political shift at the heart of Sudan's Islamist government" towards a "pragmatic engagement with the outside world," along with efforts to address Sudan's domestic crises, to end support for terrorism, and to reduce the influence of radical Islamists (Mark Huband, *Financial Times*, September 8, 1998).

Insofar as such consequences ensued, we may compare the crime in Sudan to the assassination of Lumumba, which helped plunge the Congo into decades of slaughter, still continuing; or the overthrow of the democratic government of Guatemala in 1954, which led to 40 years of hideous atrocities; and all too many others like it.

Huband's conclusions are reiterated three years later by James Astill, in the article just cited. He reviews "the political cost to a country struggling to emerge from totalitarian military dictatorship, ruinous Islamism and long-running civil war" before the missile attack, which "overnight [plunged Khartoum] into the nightmare of impotent extremism it had been trying to escape." This "political cost" may have been even more harmful to Sudan than the destruction of its "fragile medical services," he concludes.

Astill quotes Dr. Idris Eltayeb, one of Sudan's handful of pharmacologists and chairman of the board of Al-Shifa: the crime, he says, is "just as much an act of terrorism as at the Twin Towers—the only difference is we know who did it. I feel very sad about the loss of life [in New York and Washington], but in terms of numbers, and the relative cost to a poor country, [the bombing in Sudan] was worse."

Unfortunately, he may be right about "the loss of life in terms of numbers," even if we do not take into account the longer-term "political cost."

Evaluating "relative cost" is an enterprise I won't try to pursue, and it goes without saying that ranking crimes on some scale is generally ridiculous, though comparison of the toll is perfectly reasonable and indeed standard in scholarship.

The bombing also carried severe costs for the people of the United States, as became glaringly evident on September 11, or should have. It seems to me remarkable that this has not been brought up prominently (if at all), in the extensive discussion of intelligence failures that lie behind the 9-11 atrocities.

Just before the 1998 missile strike, Sudan detained two men suspected of bombing the American embassies in East Africa, notifying Washington, U.S. officials confirmed. But the U.S. rejected Sudan's offer of cooperation, and after the missile attack, Sudan "angrily released" the suspects (James Risen, *New York Times*, July 30, 1999); they have since been identified as bin Laden operatives. Recently leaked FBI memos add another reason why Sudan "angrily released" the suspects. The memos reveal that the FBI wanted them extradited, but the State Department refused. One "senior CIA source" now describes this and other rejections of Sudanese offers of cooperation as "the worst single intelligence failure in this whole terrible business" of September 11. "It is the key to the whole thing right now" because of the voluminous evidence on bin Laden that Sudan offered to produce, offers that were repeatedly rebuffed because of the administration's "irrational hatred" of Sudan, the senior CIA source reports. Included in Sudan's rejected offers was "a vast intelligence database on Osama bin Laden and more than 200 leading members of his al-Qaeda terrorist network in the years leading up to the 11 September attacks." Washington was "offered thick files, with photographs and detailed biographies of many of his principal cadres, and vital information about al-Qaeda's financial interests in many parts of the globe," but refused to accept the information, out of "irrational hatred" of the target of its missile attack. "It is reasonable to say that had we had this data we may have had a better chance of preventing the attacks" of September 11, the same senior CIA source concludes (David Rose, *Observer*, September 30, reporting an *Observer* investigation).

One can scarcely try to estimate the toll of the Sudan bombing, even apart from the probable tens of thousands of immediate Sudanese victims. The complete toll is attributable to the single act of terror—at least, if we have the honesty to adopt the standards we properly apply to official enemies. The reaction in the West tells us a lot about ourselves, if we agree to adopt another moral truism: look into the mirror.

Or to return to "our little region over here which never has bothered anybody," as Henry Stimson called the Western hemisphere, take Cuba. After many years of terror beginning in late 1959, including very serious atrocities, Cuba should have the right to resort to violence against the U.S. according to U.S. doctrine that is scarcely questioned. It is, unfortunately, all too easy to continue, not only with regard to the U.S. but also other terrorist states.

In your book Culture of Terrorism, *you write that "the cultural scene is illuminated with particular clarity by the thinking of the liberal doves, who set the limits for respectable dissent." How have they been performing since the events of September 11?*

Since I don't like to generalize, let's take a concrete example. On September 16, the *New York Times* reported that the

NOAM CHOMSKY

U.S. has demanded that Pakistan cut off food aid to Afghanistan. That had already been hinted before, but here it was stated flat out. Among other demands Washington issued to Pakistan, it also "demanded...the elimination of truck convoys that provide much of the food and other supplies to Afghanistan's civilian population"—the food that is keeping probably millions of people just this side of starvation (John Burns, Islamabad, *New York Times*). What does that mean? That means that unknown numbers of starving Afghans will die. Are these Taliban? No, they're victims of the Taliban. Many of them are internal refugees kept from leaving. But here's a statement saying, OK, let's proceed to kill unknown numbers, maybe millions, of starving Afghans who are victims of the Taliban. What was the reaction?

I spent almost the entire day afterwards on radio and television around the world. I kept bringing it up. Nobody in Europe or the U.S. could think of one word of reaction. Elsewhere in the world there was plenty of reaction, even around the periphery of Europe, like Greece. How should we have reacted to this? Suppose some power was strong enough to say, Let's do something that will cause a huge number of Americans to die of starvation. Would you think it's a serious problem? And again, it's not a fair analogy. In the case of Afghanistan, left to rot after it had been ruined by the Soviet invasion and exploited for Washington's war, much of the country is in ruins and its people are desperate, already one of the worst humanitarian crises in the world.

National Public Radio, which in the 1980s was denounced by the Reagan administration as "Radio Managua on the Potomac," is also considered "out there" on the liberal end of respectable debate. Noah Adams, the host of All Things Considered, *asked these questions on September 17: "Should assassinations be allowed? Should the CIA be given more operating leeway?"*

The CIA should not be permitted to carry out assassinations, but that's the least of it. Should the CIA be permitted to organize a car bombing in Beirut like the one I just mentioned?

Not a secret, incidentally; prominently reported in the mainstream, though easily forgotten. That didn't violate any laws. And it's not just the CIA. Should they have been permitted to organize in Nicaragua a terrorist army that had the official task, straight out of the mouth of the State Department, to attack "soft targets" in Nicaragua, meaning undefended agricultural cooperatives and health clinics? Remember that the State Department officially approved such attacks immediately after the World Court had ordered the U.S. to end its international terrorist campaign and pay substantial reparations.

What's the name for that? Or to set up something like the bin Laden network, not him himself, but the background organizations?

Should the U.S. be authorized to provide Israel with attack helicopters used to carry out political assassinations and

NOAM CHOMSKY

attacks on civilian targets? That's not the CIA. That's the Clinton administration, with no noticeable objection. In fact, it wasn't even reported, though the sources were impeccable.

Could you very briefly define the political uses of terrorism? Where does it fit in the doctrinal system?

The U.S. is officially committed to what is called "low-intensity warfare." That's the official doctrine. If you read the standard definitions of low-intensity conflict and compare them with official definitions of "terrorism" in army manuals, or the U.S. Code (see p. 16, footnote), you find they're almost the same. Terrorism is the use of coercive means aimed at civilian populations in an effort to achieve political, religious, or other aims. That's what the World Trade Center attack was, a particularly horrifying terrorist crime.

Terrorism, according to the official definitions, is simply part of state action, official doctrine, and not just that of the U.S., of course.

It is not, as is often claimed, "the weapon of the weak."

Furthermore, all of these things should be well known. It's shameful that they're not. Anybody who wants to find out about them can begin by reading the Alex George collection mentioned earlier, which runs through lots and lots of cases. These are things people need to know if they want to understand anything about themselves. They are known by the victims, of course, but the perpetrators prefer to look elsewhere.

5.

CHOICE OF ACTION

Based on an interview with Michael Albert on September 22, 2001.

Q: Let's assume, for the sake of discussion, that bin Laden was behind the events. If so, what reason might he have had? It certainly can't help poor and disempowered people anywhere, much less Palestinians, so what is his aim, if he planned the action?

CHOMSKY: One has to be cautious about this. According to Robert Fisk, who has interviewed him repeatedly and at length, Osama bin Laden shares the anger felt throughout the region at the U.S. military presence in Saudi Arabia, support for atrocities against Palestinians, along with U.S.-led devastation of Iraqi civilian society. That feeling of anger is shared by rich and poor, and across the political and other spectrums.

Many who know the conditions well are also dubious

about bin Laden's capacity to plan that incredibly sophisticated operation from a cave somewhere in Afghanistan. But that his network was involved is highly plausible, and that he is an inspiration for them, also. These are decentralized, non-hierarchic structures, probably with quite limited communication links among them. It's entirely possible that bin Laden's telling the truth when he says he didn't know about the operation.

All that aside, bin Laden is quite clear about what he wants, not only to any westerners who want to interview him, like Fisk, but more importantly to the Arabic-speaking audience that he reaches through the cassettes that circulate widely. Adopting his framework for the sake of discussion, the prime target is Saudi Arabia and other corrupt and repressive regimes of the region, none of which are truly "Islamic." And he and his network are intent on supporting Muslims defending themselves against "infidels" wherever it may be: Chechnya, Bosnia, Kashmir, Western China, Southeast Asia, North Africa, maybe elsewhere. They fought and won a Holy War to drive the Russians (Europeans who are presumably not relevantly different from British or Americans in their view) out of Muslim Afghanistan, and they are even more intent on driving the Americans out of Saudi Arabia, a far more important country to them, as it is the home of the holiest Islamic sites.

His call for the overthrow of corrupt and brutal regimes of gangsters and torturers resonates quite widely, as does his indignation against the atrocities that he and others attribute to the United States, hardly without reason. It's entirely true that his crimes are extremely harmful to the poorest and most oppressed people of the region. The latest attacks, for example, were extremely harmful to the Palestinians. But what looks like sharp inconsistency from outside may be perceived rather differently from within. By courageously fighting oppressors, who are quite real, bin Laden may appear to be a hero, however harmful his actions are to the poor majority. And if the United States succeeds in killing him, he may become even more powerful as a martyr whose voice will continue to be heard on the cassettes that are circulating and through other means. He is, after all, as much of a symbol as an objective force, both for the U.S. and probably much of the population.

There's every reason, I think, to take him at his word. And his crimes can hardly come as a surprise to the CIA. "Blowback" from the radical Islamic forces organized, armed, and trained by the U.S., Egypt, France, Pakistan, and others began almost at once, with the 1981 assassination of President Sadat of Egypt, one of the most enthusiastic of the creators of the forces assembled to fight a Holy War against the Russians. The violence has been continuing since without letup.

The blowback has been quite direct, and of a kind very familiar from 50 years of history, including the drug flow and the violence. To take one case, the leading specialist on this topic, John Cooley, reports that CIA officers "consciously assisted" the entry of the radical Islamic Egyptian cleric Sheikh Omar Abdel Rahman to the U.S. in 1990 (*Unholy Wars*). He was already wanted by Egypt on charges of terrorism. In 1993, he was implicated in the bombing of the World Trade Center, which followed procedures taught in CIA manuals that were, presumably, provided to the "Afghanis" fighting the Russians. The plan was to blow up the UN building, the Lincoln and Holland tunnels, and other targets as well. Sheikh Omar was convicted of conspiracy and given a long jail sentence.

Again, if bin Laden planned these actions, and especially if popular fears of more such actions to come are credible, what is the proper approach to reducing or eliminating the danger? What steps should be taken by the U.S. or others, domestically or internationally? What would be the results of those steps?

Every case is different, but let's take a few analogies. What was the right way for Britain to deal with IRA bombs in London? One choice would have been to send the RAF to bomb the source of their finances, places like Boston, or to infiltrate commandos to capture those suspected of involvement in such financing and kill them or spirit them to London to face trial.

Putting aside feasibility, that would have been criminal idiocy. Another possibility was to consider realistically the background concerns and grievances, and to try to remedy them, while at the same time following the rule of law to punish criminals. That would make a lot more sense, one would think. Or take the bombing of the federal building in Oklahoma City. There were immediate calls for bombing the Middle East, and it probably would have happened if even a remote hint of a link had been found. When it was instead discovered to be a domestically devised attack, by someone with militia connections, there was no call to obliterate Montana and Idaho, or the "Republic of Texas," which has been calling for secession from the oppressive and illegitimate government in Washington. Rather, there was a search for the perpetrator, who was found, brought to court, and sentenced, and to the extent that the reaction was sensible, there were efforts to understand the grievances that lie behind such crimes and to address the problems. At least, that is the course we follow if we have any concern for genuine justice and hope to reduce the likelihood of further atrocities rather than increase it. The same principles hold quite generally, with due attention to variation of circumstances. Specifically, they hold in this case.

What steps, in contrast, is the U.S. government seeking to undertake? What will be the results, if they succeed in their plans?

What has been announced is a virtual declaration of war against all who do not join Washington in its resort to violence, however it chooses.

The nations of the world face a "stark choice": join us in

our crusade or "face the certain prospect of death and destruction" (R. W. Apple, *New York Times*, September 14). Bush's rhetoric of September 20 forcefully reiterates that stance. Taken literally, it's virtually a declaration of war against much of the world. But I am sure we should not take it literally. Government planners do not want to undermine their own interests so grievously. What their actual plans are, we do not know. But I suppose they will take to heart the warnings they are receiving from foreign leaders, specialists in the region, and presumably their own intelligence agencies that a massive military assault, which would kill many innocent civilians, would be exactly "what the perpetrators of the Manhattan slaughter must want above all. Military retaliation would elevate their cause, idolize their leader, devalue moderation and validate fanaticism. If ever history needed a catalyst for a new and awful conflict between Arabs and the West, this could be it" (Simon Jenkins, *Times* [London], September 14, one of many who made these points insistently from the outset).

Even if bin Laden is killed—maybe even more so if he is killed—a slaughter of innocents would only intensify the feelings of anger, desperation and frustration that are rampant in the region, and mobilize others to his horrendous cause.

What the administration does will depend, in part at least, on the mood at home, which we can hope to influence. What the consequences of their actions will be we cannot say with much confidence, any more than they can. But there are plausible estimates, and unless the course of reason, law, and treaty obligations is pursued, the prospects could be quite grim.

Many people say that the citizens of Arab nations should have taken responsibility to remove terrorists from the planet, or governments that support terrorists. How do you react?

It makes sense to call upon citizens to eliminate terrorists instead of electing them to high office, lauding and rewarding them. But I would not suggest that we should have "removed our elected officials, their advisers, their intellectual claque, and their clients from the planet," or destroyed our own and other Western governments because of their terrorist crimes and their support for terrorists worldwide, including many who were transferred from favored friends and allies to the category of "terrorists" because they disobeyed U.S. orders: Saddam Hussein, and many others like him. However, it is rather unfair to blame citizens of harsh and brutal regimes that we support for not undertaking this responsibility, when we do not do so under vastly more propitious circumstances.

Many people say that all through history when a nation is attacked, it attacks in kind. How do you react?

When countries are attacked they try to defend themselves, if they can. According to the doctrine proposed, Nicaragua,

South Vietnam, Cuba, and numerous others should have been setting off bombs in Washington and other U.S. cities, Palestinians should be applauded for bombings in Tel Aviv, and on and on. It is because such doctrines had brought Europe to virtual self-annihilation after hundreds of years of savagery that the nations of the world forged a different compact after World War II, establishing—at least formally—the principle that the resort to force is barred except in the case of self-defense against armed attack until the Security Council acts to protect international peace and security. Specifically, retaliation is barred. Since the U.S. is not under armed attack, in the sense of Article 51 of the UN Charter, these considerations are irrelevant—at least, if we agree that the fundamental principles of international law should apply to ourselves, not only to those we dislike.

International law aside, we have centuries of experience that tell us exactly what is entailed by the doctrines now being proposed and hailed by many commentators. In a world with weapons of mass destruction, what it entails is an imminent termination of the human experiment—which is, after all, why Europeans decided half a century ago that the game of mutual slaughter in which they had been indulging for centuries had better come to an end, or else.

In the immediate aftermath of 9-11, many people were horrified to see expressions of anger at the U.S. emanating from various parts of the world, including but not confined to the Middle East. Images of people celebrating the

NOAM CHOMSKY

destruction of the World Trade Center leave people want-
ing revenge. How do you react to that?

A U.S.-backed army took control in Indonesia in 1965, organizing the slaughter of hundreds of thousands of people, mostly landless peasants, in a massacre that the CIA compared to the crimes of Hitler, Stalin, and Mao. The massacre, accurately reported, elicited uncontrolled euphoria in the West, in the national media and elsewhere. Indonesian peasants had not harmed us in any way. When Nicaragua finally succumbed to the U.S. assault, the mainstream press lauded the success of the methods adopted to "wreck the economy and prosecute a long and deadly proxy war until the exhausted natives overthrow the unwanted government themselves," with a cost to us that is "minimal," leaving the victims "with wrecked bridges, sabotaged power stations, and ruined farms," and thus providing the U.S. candidate with "a winning issue": ending the "impoverishment of the people of Nicaragua" (*Time*). We are "United in Joy" at this outcome, the *New York Times* proclaimed. It's easy to continue.

Very few people around the world celebrated the crimes in New York; overwhelmingly, the atrocities were passionately deplored, even in places where people have been ground underfoot by Washington's boots for a long, long time. But there were undoubtedly feelings of anger at the United States. However, I am aware of nothing as grotesque as the two examples I just mentioned, or many more like them in the West.

Getting beyond these public reactions, in your view what are the actual motivations operating in U.S. policy at this moment? What is the purpose of the "war on terror," as proposed by Bush?

The "war on terror" is neither new nor a "war on terror." We should recall that the Reagan administration came to office 20 years ago proclaiming that "international terrorism" (sponsored worldwide by the Soviet Union) is the greatest threat faced by the U.S., which is the main target of terrorism, and its allies and friends. We must therefore dedicate ourselves to a war to eradicate this "cancer," this "plague" that is destroying civilization. The Reaganites acted on that commitment by organizing campaigns of international terrorism that were extraordinary in scale and destruction, even leading to a World Court condemnation of the U.S., while lending their support to innumerable others, for example, in southern Africa, where Western-backed South African depredations killed a million and a half people and caused $60 billion of damage during the Reagan years alone. Hysteria over international terrorism peaked in the mid-80s, while the U.S. and its allies were well in the lead in spreading the cancer they were demanding must be extirpated.

If we choose, we can live in a world of comforting illusion. Or we can look at recent history, at the institutional structures that remain essentially unchanged, at the plans that are being announced—and answer the questions accordingly. I know of no reason to suppose that there has been a sudden change in long-standing motivations or policy goals, apart from tactical adjustments to changing circumstances.

We should also remember that one exalted task of intellectuals is to proclaim every few years that we have "changed course," the past is behind us and can be forgotten as we march on towards a glorious future. That is a highly convenient stance, though hardly an admirable or sensible one.

The literature on all this is voluminous. There is no reason, beyond choice, to remain unaware of the facts—which are, of course, familiar to the victims, though few of them are in a position to recognize the scale or nature of the international terrorist assault to which they are subjected.

Do you believe that most Americans will, as conditions permit more detailed evaluation of options, accept that the solution to terror attacks on civilians here is for the U.S. to respond with terror attacks against civilians abroad, and that the solution to fanaticism is surveillance and curtailed civil liberties?

I hope not, but we should not underestimate the capacity of well-run propaganda systems to drive people to irrational, murderous, and suicidal behavior. Take an example that is remote enough so that we should be able to look at it with some dispassion: World War I. It can't have been that both sides were engaged in a noble war for the highest objectives.

But on both sides, the soldiers marched off to mutual slaughter with enormous exuberance, fortified by the cheers of the intellectual classes and those who they helped mobilize, across the political spectrum, from left to right, including the most powerful left political force in the world, in Germany. Exceptions are so few that we can practically list them, and some of the most prominent among them ended up in jail for questioning the nobility of the enterprise: among them Rosa Luxemburg, Bertrand Russell, and Eugene Debs. With the help of Wilson's propaganda agencies and the enthusiastic support of liberal intellectuals, a pacifist country was turned in a few months into raving anti-German hysterics, ready to take revenge on those who had perpetrated savage crimes, many of them invented by the British Ministry of Information. But that's by no means inevitable, and we should not underestimate the civilizing effects of the popular struggles of recent years. We need not stride resolutely towards catastrophe, merely because those are the marching orders.

NOAM CHOMSKY

6.

CIVILIZATIONS EAST AND WEST

Based on interviews with European media September 20-22, 2001 with
Marili Margomenou for Alpha TV Station (Greece), Miguel Mora for *El País*
(Spain), Natalie Levisalles for *Liberation* (France).

[*Editor's note: As many of these questions were written by journalists who speak English as a second language, in some instances phrases were edited for clarity with every effort to preserve the intended meaning.*]

Q: *After the attack in the U.S.A., Secretary of State Colin L. Powell said that the U.S. government will revise the laws for terrorism, including the law of 1976 that prohibits assassinations of foreigners. The European Union is also about to apply a new law on terrorism. How might response to the attacks come to constrict our freedoms? For instance, does terrorism give government the right to put us under surveillance, in order to trace suspects and prevent future attacks?*

CHOMSKY: A response that is too abstract may be misleading, so let us consider a current and quite typical illustration of what plans to relax constraints on state violence mean in practice. This morning (September 21), the *New York Times* ran an opinion piece by Michael Walzer, a respected intellectual who is considered a moral leader. He called for an "ideological campaign to engage all the arguments and excuses for terrorism and reject them"; since, as he knows, there are no such arguments and excuses for terrorism of the kind he has in mind, at least on the part of anyone amenable to reason, in effect this translates as a call to reject efforts to explore the reasons that lie behind terrorist acts that are directed against states he supports. He then proceeds, in conventional fashion, to enlist himself among those who provide "arguments and excuses for terrorism," tacitly endorsing political assassination, namely, Israeli assassinations of Palestinians who Israel claims support terrorism; no evidence is offered or considered necessary, and in many cases even the suspicions appear groundless. And the inevitable "collateral damage"—women, children, others nearby—is treated in the standard way. U.S.-supplied attack helicopters have been used for such assassinations for 10 months.

Walzer puts the word "assassination" in quotes, indicating that in his view, the term is part of what he calls the "fervid and highly distorted accounts of the blockade of Iraq and the Israeli-Palestinian conflict." He is referring to criticism of U.S.-backed Israeli atrocities in the territories that have been under harsh and brutal military occupation for almost 35 years, and of U.S. policies that have devastated the civilian society of Iraq (while strengthening Saddam Hussein). Such criticisms are marginal in the U.S., but too much for him, apparently. By "distorted accounts," perhaps Walzer has in mind occasional references to the statement of Secretary of State Madeleine Albright over national TV when she was asked about the estimates of a half million deaths of Iraqi children as a result of the sanctions regime. She recognized that such consequences were a "hard choice" for her administration, but said "we think the price is worth it."

I mention this single example, easily multiplied, to illustrate the substantive meaning of the relaxation of constraints on state action. We may recall that violent and murderous states quite commonly justify their actions as "counter-terrorism": for example, the Nazis fighting partisan resistance. And such actions are commonly justified by respected intellectuals.

That is not ancient history. In December 1987, at the peak of concern over international terrorism, the UN General Assembly passed its major resolution on the matter, condemning the plague in the strongest terms and calling on all nations to act forcefully to overcome it. The resolution passed 153-2 (U.S. and Israel), Honduras alone abstaining. The offending passage states "that nothing in the present resolution could in any way prejudice the right to self-determination, freedom and independence, as derived from the Charter of the United Nations, of peoples forcibly deprived of that right..., particularly peoples under colonial and racist regimes and foreign occupation or other forms of colonial domination, nor...the right of these peoples to struggle to this end and to seek and receive support [in accordance with the Charter and other principles of international law]." These rights are not accepted by the U.S. and Israel; or at the time, their South African ally. For Washington, the African

National Congress was a "terrorist organization," but South Africa did not join Cuba and others as a "terrorist state. "Washington's interpretation of "terrorism" of course prevails, in practice, with human consequences that have been severe.

There is now much talk about formulating a Comprehensive Convention against Terrorism, no small task. The reason, carefully skirted in reports, is that the U.S. will not accept anything like the offending passage of the 1987 resolution, and none of its allies will accept it either if the definition of "terrorism" conforms to official definitions in the U.S. Code or army manuals, but only if it can somehow be reshaped to exclude the terrorism of the powerful and their clients.

To be sure, there are many factors to be considered in thinking about your question. But the historical record is of overwhelming importance. At a very general level, the question cannot be answered. It depends on specific circumstances and specific proposals.

Bundestag in Germany already decided that German soldiers will join American forces, although 80 percent of the German people do not agree with this, according to a survey of the Forsa Institute. What are your thoughts on this?

For the moment, European powers are hesitant about joining Washington's crusade, fearing that by a massive assault against innocent civilians the U.S. will provide bin Laden, or others like him, with a way to mobilize desperate and angry people to their cause, with consequences that could be even more horrifying.

What do you think about nations acting as a global community during a time of war? It is not the first time that every country must ally with the U.S.A., or be considered an enemy, but now Afghanistan is declaring the same thing.

The Bush administration at once presented the nations of the world with a choice: join us, or face destruction. [*Editor's note: Here Chomsky is referring to a quote published in the* New York Times, *September 14, 2001. See page 64.*]

The "global community" strongly opposes terror, including the massive terror of the powerful states, and also the terrible crimes of September 11. But the "global community" does not act. When Western states and intellectuals use the term "international community," they are referring to themselves. For example, NATO bombing of Serbia was undertaken by the "international community" according to consistent Western rhetoric, although those who did not have their heads buried in the sand knew that it was opposed by most of the world, often quite vocally. Those who do not support the actions of wealth and power are not part of "the global community," just as "terrorism" conventionally means "terrorism directed against us and our friends."

It is hardly surprising that Afghanistan is attempting to mimic the U.S., calling on Muslims for support. The scale, of course, is vastly smaller. Even as remote as they are from the world outside, Taliban leaders presumably know full well that the Islamic states are not their friends. These states have, in fact, been subjected to terrorist attack by the radical Islamist forces that were organized and trained to fight a Holy War against the U.S.S.R. 20 years ago, and began to pursue their own terrorist agenda elsewhere immediately, with the assassination of Egyptian president Sadat.

According to you, an attack against Afghanistan is a "war against terrorism"?

An attack against Afghanistan will probably kill a great many innocent civilians, possibly enormous numbers in a country where millions are already on the verge of death from starvation. Wanton killing of innocent civilians is terrorism, not a war against terrorism.

Could you imagine how the situation would be if the terrorist's attack in the U.S.A. had happened during the night, when very few people would be in the WTC? In other words, if there were very few victims, would the American government react in the same way? Up to what point is it influenced by the symbolism of this disaster, the fact that it was the Pentagon and the Twin Towers that were hit?

I doubt that it would have made any difference. It would have been a terrible crime even if the toll had been much smaller. The Pentagon is more than a "symbol," for reasons that need no comment. As for the World Trade Center, we scarcely know what the terrorists had in mind when they bombed it in 1993 and destroyed it on September 11. But we can be quite confident that it had little to do with such matters as "globalization," or "economic imperialism," or "cultural values," matters that are utterly unfamiliar to bin Laden and his associates, or other radical Islamists like those convicted for the 1993 bombings, and of no concern to them, just as they are, evidently, not concerned by the fact that their atrocities over the years have caused great harm to poor and oppressed people in the Muslim world and elsewhere, again on September 11.

Among the immediate victims are Palestinians under military occupation, as the perpetrators surely must have known. Their concerns are different, and bin Laden, at least, has been eloquent enough in expressing them in many interviews: to overthrow the corrupt and repressive regimes of the Arab world and replace them with properly "Islamic" regimes, to support Muslims in their struggles against "infidels" in Saudi Arabia (which he regards as under U.S. occupation), Chechnya, Bosnia, western China, North Africa, and Southeast Asia; maybe elsewhere.

It is convenient for Western intellectuals to speak of "deeper causes" such as hatred of Western values and progress. That is a useful way to avoid questions about the origin of the bin Laden network itself, and about the practices that lead to anger, fear, and desperation throughout the region, and provide a reservoir from which radical Islamic terrorist cells can sometimes draw. Since the answers to these questions are rather clear, and are inconsistent with preferred doctrine, it is better to dismiss the questions as "superficial" and "insignificant," and to turn to "deeper causes" that are in fact more superficial, even insofar as they are relevant.

Should we call what is happening now a war?

There is no precise definition of "war." People speak of the "war on poverty," the "drug war," etc. What is taking shape is not a conflict among states, though it could become one.

Can we talk of the clash between two civilizations?

This is fashionable talk, but it makes little sense. Suppose we briefly review some familiar history. The most populous Islamic state is Indonesia, a favorite of the United States ever since Suharto took power in 1965, as army-led massacres slaughtered hundreds of thousands of people, mostly landless peasants, with the assistance of the U.S. and with an outburst of euphoria from the West that is so embarrassing in retrospect that it has been effectively wiped out of memory. Suharto remained "our kind of guy," as the Clinton administration called him, as he compiled one of the most horrendous records of slaughter, torture, and other abuses of the late 20th century. The most extreme Islamic fundamentalist state, apart from the Taliban, is Saudi Arabia, a U.S. client since its founding. In the 1980s, the U.S. along with Pakistani intelligence (helped by Saudi Arabia, Britain, and others), recruited, armed, and trained the most extreme Islamic fundamentalists they could find to cause maximal harm to the Soviets in Afghanistan. As Simon Jenkins observes in the London *Times*, those efforts "destroyed a moderate regime and created a fanatical one, from groups recklessly financed by the Americans" (most of the funding was probably Saudi). One of the indirect beneficiaries was Osama bin Laden.

Also in the 1980s, the U.S. and U.K. gave strong support to their friend and ally Saddam Hussein—more secular, to be sure, but on the Islamic side of the "clash"—right through the period of his worst atrocities, including the gassing of the Kurds, and beyond.

Also in the 1980s the U.S. fought a major war in Central America, leaving some 200,000 tortured and mutilated corpses, millions of orphans and refugees, and four countries devastated. A prime target of the U.S. attack was the Catholic Church, which had committed the grievous sin of adopting "the preferential option for the poor."

In the early 90s, primarily for cynical power reasons, the U.S. selected Bosnian Muslims as their Balkan clients, hardly to their benefit.

Without continuing, exactly where do we find the divide

between "civilizations." Are we to conclude that there is a "clash of civilizations" with the Latin American Catholic Church on one side, and the U.S. and the Muslim world, including its most murderous and fanatic religious elements, on the other side? I do not of course suggest any such absurdity. But exactly what are we to conclude, on rational grounds?

Do you think we are using the word "civilization" properly? Would a really civilized world lead us to a global war like this?

No civilized society would tolerate anything I have just mentioned, which is of course only a tiny sample even of U.S. history, and European history is even worse. And surely no "civilized world" would plunge the world into a major war instead of following the means prescribed by international law, following ample precedents.

The attacks have been called an act of hate. Where do you think this hate comes from?

For the radical Islamists mobilized by the CIA and its associates, the hate is just what they express. The U.S. was happy to support their hatred and violence when it was directed against U.S. enemies; it is not happy when the hatred it helped nurture is directed against the U.S. and its allies, as it has been, repeatedly, for 20 years. For the population of the region, quite a distinct category, the reasons for their feelings are not obscure. The sources of those sentiments are also quite well known.

What do you suggest the citizens of the Western world could do to bring back peace?

That depends what these citizens want. If they want an escalating cycle of violence, in the familiar pattern, they should certainly call on the U.S. to fall into bin Laden's "diabolical trap" and massacre innocent civilians. If they want to reduce the level of violence, they should use their influence to direct the great powers in a very different course, the one I outlined earlier, which, again, has ample precedents. That includes a willingness to examine what lies behind the atrocities. One often hears that we must not consider these matters, because that would be justification for terrorism, a position so foolish and destructive as scarcely to merit comment, but unfortunately common. But if we do not wish to contribute to escalating the cycle of violence, with targets among the rich and powerful as well, that is exactly what we must do, as in all other cases, including those familiar enough in Spain. [*Editor's note: Chomsky is being interviewed by the Spanish press, and thus his references to Spain.*]

Did the U.S. "ask for" these attacks? Are they consequences of American politics?

The attacks are not "consequences" of U.S. policies in any direct sense. But indirectly, of course they are consequences; that is not even controversial. There seems little doubt that the perpetrators come from the terrorist network that has its roots in the mercenary armies that were organized, trained, and armed by the CIA, Egypt, Pakistan, French intelligence, Saudi Arabian funding, and others. The backgrounds of all of this remain somewhat murky. The organization of these forces started in 1979, if we can believe President Carter's National Security Adviser Zbigniew Brzezinski. He claimed, maybe he was just bragging, that in mid-1979 he had instigated secret support for Mujahidin fighting against the government of Afghanistan in an effort to draw the Russians into what he called an "Afghan trap," a phrase worth remembering. He's very proud of the fact that they did fall into the "Afghan trap" by sending military forces to support the government six months later, with consequences that we know. The United States, along with its allies, assembled a huge mercenary army, maybe 100,000 or more, and they drew from the most militant sectors they could find, which happened to be radical Islamists, what are called here Islamic fundamentalists, from all over, most of them not from Afghanistan. They're called "Afghanis," but like bin Laden, many come from elsewhere.

Bin Laden joined sometime in the 1980s. He was involved in the funding networks, which probably are the ones which still exist. They fought a holy war against the Russian occupiers. They carried terror into Russian territory. They won the war and the Russian invaders withdrew. The war was not their only activity. In 1981, forces based in those same groups assassinated President Sadat of Egypt, who had been instrumental in setting them up. In 1983, one suicide bomber, maybe with connections to the same forces, essentially drove the U.S. military out of Lebanon. And it continued.

By 1989, they had succeeded in their Holy War in Afghanistan. As soon as the U.S. established a permanent military presence in Saudi Arabia, bin Laden and the rest announced that from their point of view, that was comparable to the Russian occupation of Afghanistan and they turned their guns on the Americans, as had already happened in 1983 when the U.S. had military forces in Lebanon. Saudi Arabia is a major enemy of the bin Laden network, just as Egypt is. That's what they want to overthrow, what they call the un-Islamic governments of Egypt, Saudi Arabia, other states of the Middle East, and North Africa. And it continued.

In 1997 they murdered roughly sixty tourists in Egypt and destroyed the Egyptian tourist industry. And they've been carrying out activities all over the region, North Africa, East Africa, the Middle East, the Balkans, Central Asia, western China, Southeast Asia, the U.S., for years. That's one group. And that is an outgrowth of the wars of the 1980s and, if you can believe Brzezinski, even before, when they set the "Afghan trap." Furthermore, as is common knowledge among anyone who pays attention to the region, the terrorists draw from a reservoir of desperation, anger, and frustration that extends from rich to poor, from secular to radical Islamist. That it is rooted in no small measure in U.S. policies is evident and constantly articulated to those willing to listen.

You said that the main practitioners of terrorism are countries like the U.S. that use violence for political motives. When and where?

I find the question baffling. As I've said elsewhere, the U.S. is, after all, the only country condemned by the World Court for international terrorism—for "the unlawful use of force" for political ends, as the Court put it—ordering the U.S. to terminate these crimes and pay substantial reparations. The U.S. of course dismissed the Court's judgment with contempt, reacting by escalating the terrorist war against Nicaragua and vetoing a Security Council resolution calling on all states to observe international law (and voting alone, with Israel and in one case El Salvador, against similar General Assembly resolutions). The terrorist war expanded in accordance with the official policy of attacking "soft targets"—undefended civilian targets, like agricultural collectives and health clinics—instead of engaging the Nicaraguan army. The terrorists were able to carry out these instructions, thanks to the complete control of Nicaraguan air space by the U.S. and the advanced communications equipment provided to them by their supervisors.

It should also be recognized that these terrorist actions were widely approved. One prominent commentator,

Michael Kinsley, at the liberal extreme of the mainstream, argued that we should not simply dismiss State Department justifications for terrorist attacks on "soft targets": a "sensible policy" must "meet the test of cost-benefit analysis," he wrote, an analysis of "the amount of blood and misery that will be poured in, and the likelihood that democracy will emerge at the other end"—"democracy" as the U.S. understands the term, an interpretation illustrated quite clearly in the region. It is taken for granted that U.S. elites have the right to conduct the analysis and pursue the project if it passes their tests.

Even more dramatically, the idea that Nicaragua should have the right to defend itself was considered outrageous across the mainstream political spectrum in the United States. The U.S. pressured allies to stop providing Nicaragua with arms, hoping that it would turn to Russia, as it did; that provides the right propaganda images. The Reagan administration repeatedly floated rumors that Nicaragua was receiving jet fighters from Russia—to protect its airspace, as everyone knew, and to prevent U.S. terrorist attacks against "soft targets." The rumors were false, but the reaction was instructive. The doves questioned the rumors, but said that if they are true, of course we must bomb Nicaragua, because it will be a threat to our security. Database searches revealed that there was scarcely a hint that Nicaragua had the right to defend itself. That tells us quite a lot about the deep-seated "culture of terrorism" that prevails in Western civilization.

This is by no means the most extreme example; I mention it because it is uncontroversial, given the World Court decision, and because the failed efforts of Nicaragua to pursue lawful means, instead of setting off bombs in Washington, provide a model for today, not the only one. Nicaragua was only one component of Washington's terrorist wars in Central America in that terrible decade, leaving hundreds of thousands dead and four countries in ruins.

During the same years the U.S. was carrying out large-scale terrorism elsewhere, including the Middle East: to cite one example, the car bombing in Beirut in 1985 outside a mosque, timed to kill the maximum number of civilians, with 80 dead and 250 casualties, aimed at a Muslim sheikh, who escaped. And it supported much worse terror: for example, Israel's invasion of Lebanon that killed some 18,000 Lebanese and Palestinian civilians, not in self-defense, as was conceded at once; and the vicious "iron fist" atrocities of the years that followed, directed against "terrorist villagers," as Israel put it. And the subsequent invasions of 1993 and 1996, both strongly supported by the U.S. (until the international reaction to the Qana massacre in 1996, which caused Clinton to draw back). The post-1982 toll in Lebanon alone is probably another 20,000 civilians.

In the 1990s, the U.S. provided 80 percent of the arms for Turkey's counterinsurgency campaign against Kurds in its southeast region, killing tens of thousands, driving 2-3 million out of their homes, leaving 3,500 villages destroyed (7 times Kosovo under NATO bombs), and with every imaginable atrocity. The arms flow had increased sharply in 1984 as Turkey launched its terrorist attack and began to decline to previous levels only in 1999, when the atrocities had achieved their goal. In 1999, Turkey fell from its position as the leading recipient of U.S. arms (Israel-Egypt aside), replaced by Colombia, the worst human rights violator in the hemisphere in the 1990s and by far the leading recipient of U.S. arms and training, following a consistent pattern.

In East Timor, the U.S. (and Britain) continued their support of the Indonesian aggressors, who had already wiped out about 1/3 of the population with their crucial help. That continued right through the atrocities of 1999, with thousands murdered even before the early September assault that drove 85 percent of the population from their homes and destroyed 70 percent of the country—while the Clinton administration kept to its position that "it is the responsibility of the government of Indonesia, and we don't want to take that responsibility away from them."

That was September 8, well after the worst of the September atrocities had been reported. By then Clinton was coming under enormous pressure to do something to mitigate the atrocities, mainly from Australia but also from home. A few days later, the Clinton administration indicated to the Indonesian generals that the game was over. They instantly reversed course. They had been strongly insisting that they would never withdraw from East Timor, and they were in fact setting up defenses in Indonesian West Timor (using British jets, which Britain continued to send) to repel a possible intervention force. When Clinton gave the word, they reversed course 180 degrees and announced that they would withdraw, allowing an Australian-led UN peacekeeping force to enter unopposed by the army. The course of events reveals very graphically the latent power that was always available to Washington, and that could have been used to prevent 25 years of virtual genocide culminating in the new wave of atrocities from early 1999. Instead, successive U.S. administrations, joined by Britain and others in 1978 when atrocities were peaking, preferred to lend crucial support, military and diplomatic, to the killers—to "our kind of guy," as the Clinton administration described the murderous President Suharto. These facts, clear and dramatic, identify starkly the prime locus of responsibility for these terrible crimes of 25 years—in fact, continuing in miserable refugee camps in Indonesian West Timor.

We also learn a lot about Western civilization from the fact that this shameful record is hailed as evidence of our new dedication to "humanitarian intervention," and a justification for the NATO bombing of Serbia.

I have already mentioned the devastation of Iraqi civilian society, with about 1 million deaths, over half of them young children, according to reports that cannot simply be ignored.

This is only a small sample.

I am, frankly, surprised that the question can even be raised—particularly in France, which has made its own contributions to massive state terror and violence, surely not unfamiliar. [*Editor's note: Chomsky is being interviewed by French media here, thus the references to France.*]

Are reactions unanimous in the U.S.? Do you share them, partly or completely?

If you mean the reaction of outrage over the horrifying criminal assault, and sympathy for the victims, then the reactions are virtually unanimous everywhere, including the Muslim countries. Of course every sane person shares them completely, not "partly." If you are referring to the calls for a murderous assault that will surely kill many innocent people—and, incidentally, answer bin Laden's most fervent prayers—than there is no such "unanimous reaction," despite superficial impressions that one might derive from watching TV. As for me, I join a great many others in opposing such actions. A great many.

What majority sentiment is, no one can really say: it is too diffuse and complex. But "unanimous"? Surely not, except with regard to the nature of the crime.

Do you condemn terrorism? How can we decide which act is terrorism and which one is an act of resistance against a tyrant or an occupying force? In which category do you "classify" the recent strike against the U.S.A.?

I understand the term "terrorism" exactly in the sense defined in official U.S. documents: "the calculated use of violence or threat of violence to attain goals that are political, religious, or ideological in nature. This is done through intimidation, coercion, or instilling fear." In accord with this—entirely appropriate—definition, the recent attack on the U.S. is certainly an act of terrorism; in fact, a horrifying terrorist crime. There is scarcely any disagreement about this throughout the world, nor should there be.

But alongside the literal meaning of the term, as just quoted from U.S. official documents, there is also a propagandistic usage, which unfortunately is the standard one: the term "terrorism" is used to refer to terrorist acts committed by enemies against us or our allies. This propagandistic use is virtually universal. Everyone "condemns terrorism" in this sense of the term. Even the Nazis harshly condemned terrorism and carried out what they called "counter-terrorism" against the terrorist partisans.

The United States basically agreed. It organized and conducted similar "counter-terrorism" in Greece and elsewhere in the postwar years. [Editor's note: The interviewer here is a Greek journalist, thus Chomsky's references to Greece.] Furthermore, U.S. counterinsurgency programs drew quite explicitly from the Nazi model, which was treated with respect: Wehrmacht officers were consulted and their manuals were used in designing postwar counterinsurgency programs worldwide, typically called "counter-terrorism," matters studied in important work by Michael McClintock, in particular. Given these conventions, even the very same people and actions can quickly shift from "terrorists" to

NOAM CHOMSKY

"freedom fighters" and back again. That's been happening right next door to Greece in recent years.

The KLA-UCK were officially condemned by the U.S. as "terrorists" in 1998, because of their attacks on Serb police and civilians in an effort to elicit a disproportionate and brutal Serbian response, as they openly declared. As late as January 1999, the British—the most hawkish element in NATO on this matter—believed that the KLA-UCK was responsible for more deaths than Serbia, which is hard to believe, but at least tells us something about perceptions at high levels in NATO. If one can trust the voluminous documentation provided by the State Department, NATO, the OSCE, and other Western sources, nothing materially changed on the ground until the withdrawal of the KVM monitors and the bombing in late March 1999. But policies did change: the U.S. and U.K. decided to launch an attack on Serbia, and the "terrorists" instantly became "freedom fighters." After the war, the "freedom fighters" and their close associates became "terrorists," "thugs," and "murderers" as they carried out what from their point of view are similar actions for similar reasons in Macedonia, a U.S. ally.

Everyone condemns terrorism, but we have to ask what they mean. You can find the answer to your question about my views in many books and articles that I have written about terrorism in the past several decades, though I use the term in the literal sense, and hence condemn all terrorist actions, not only those that are called "terrorist" for propagandistic reasons.

Is Islam dangerous to Western civilization? Does the Western way of life pose a threat to mankind?

The question is too broad and vague for me to answer. It should be clear, however, that the U.S. does not regard Islam as an enemy, or conversely.

As for the "Western way of life," it includes a great variety of elements, many highly admirable, many adopted with enthusiasm in the Islamic world, many criminal and even a threat to human survival.

As for "Western civilization," perhaps we can heed the words attributed to Gandhi when asked what he thought about "Western civilization": he said that it might be a good idea.

7.

CONSIDERABLE RESTRAINT?

Based on interviews with Michael Albert on September 30, 2001,
and Greg Ruggiero on October 5, 2001.

Q: There has been an immense movement of troops and extreme use of military rhetoric, up to comments about terminating governments, etc. Yet, now there appears to be considerable restraint...what happened?

CHOMSKY: From the first days after the attack, the Bush administration has been warned by NATO leaders, specialists on the region, and presumably its own intelligence agencies (not to speak of many people like you and me) that if they react with a massive assault that kills many innocent people, they will be fulfilling the ardent wishes of bin Laden and others like him. That would be true—perhaps even more so—if they happen to kill bin Laden, still without having provided credible evidence of his involvement in the crimes of September 11. He would then be perceived as a martyr even among the enormous majority of Muslims who deplore those crimes. If he is silenced by imprisonment or death, his voice will continue to resound on tens of thousands of cassettes already circulating throughout the Muslim world, and in many interviews, including late September. An assault that kills innocent Afghans would be virtually a call for new recruits to the horrendous cause of the bin Laden network and other graduates of the terrorist forces set up by the CIA and its associates 20 years ago to fight a Holy War against the Russians, meanwhile following their own agenda.

The message appears to have finally gotten through to the Bush administration, which has—wisely from their point of view—chosen to follow a different course.

However, "restraint" seems to me a questionable word. On September 16, the *New York Times* reported that "Washington has also demanded [from Pakistan] a cutoff of fuel supplies...and the elimination of truck convoys that provide much of the food and other supplies to Afghanistan's civilian population." Remarkably, that report elicited no detectable reaction in the West, a grim reminder of the nature of the Western civilization that leaders and intellectual elites claim to uphold. In the following days, those demands were implemented. On September 27, the same correspondent reported that officials in Pakistan "said today that they would not relent in their decision to seal off the country's 1,400-mile border with Afghanistan, a move requested by the Bush administration because, the officials said, they wanted to be sure that none of Mr. bin Laden's men were hiding among the huge tide of refugees" (John Burns, Islamabad). "The threat of military strikes forced the removal of international aid workers, crippling assistance programs"; refugees reaching Pakistan "after arduous journeys from Afghanistan are describing scenes of desperation and fear at home as the threat of American-led military attacks turns their long-running misery into a potential catastrophe" (Douglas Frantz, *New York Times*, September 30). "The country was on a lifeline," one evacuated aid worker reports, "and we just cut the line" (John Sifton, *New York Times Magazine*, September 30).

According to the world's leading newspaper, then, Washington acted at once to ensure the death and suffering of enormous numbers of Afghans, millions of them already on the brink of starvation. That is the meaning of the words just quoted, and many others like them.

Huge numbers of miserable people have been fleeing to the borders in terror after Washington's threat to bomb the shreds of existence remaining in Afghanistan and to convert the Northern Alliance into a heavily armed military force. They naturally fear that if these forces are unleashed, now greatly reinforced, they might renew the atrocities that tore the country apart and led much of the population to welcome the Taliban when they drove out the murderous warring factions that Washington and Moscow now hope to exploit for their own purposes.

Their record is atrocious. The executive director of the

arms division at Human rights Watch, Joost Hiltermann, a Middle East specialist, describes the period of their rule from 1992 to 1995 as "the worst in Afghanistan's history." Human Rights groups report that their warring factions killed tens of thousands of civilians, also committing mass rapes and other atrocities. That continued as they were driven out by the Taliban. To take one case, in 1997 they murdered 3000 prisoners of war, according to HRW, and they have also carried out massive ethnic cleansing in areas suspected of Taliban sympathies, leaving a trail of burned-out villages (see, among others, Charles Sennott, *Boston Globe*, October 6).

There is also every reason to suppose that Taliban terror, already awful enough, sharply increased in response to the same expectations that caused the refugee flight.

When they reach the sealed borders, refugees are trapped to die in silence. Only a trickle can escape through remote mountain passes. How many have already succumbed we cannot guess. Within a few weeks the harsh winter will arrive. There are some reporters and aid workers in the refugee camps across the borders. What they describe is horrifying enough, but they know, and we know, that they are seeing the lucky ones, the few who were able to escape—and who express their hopes that "even the cruel Americans must feel some pity for our ruined country" and relent in this silent genocide (*Boston Globe*, September 27, page 1).

The UN World Food Program was able to truck hundreds of tons of food into Afghanistan in early October, though it estimated that this accounted for only 15 percent of the country's needs after the withdrawal of the international staff and the three-week break in deliveries following 9-11. However, the WFP announced that it halted all food convoys and all distribution of food by its local staff because of the air strikes of October 7. "The nightmare scenario of up to 1.5 million refugees flooding out of the country moved a step closer to reality" after the attacks, AFP reported, citing aid officials. A WFP director said that after the bombing, the threat of humanitarian catastrophe, already severe, had "increased on a scale of magnitude I don't even want to think about." "We are facing a humanitarian crisis of epic proportions in Afghanistan with 7.5 million short of food and at risk of starvation," a spokesman for the UNHCR warned. All agencies regard air drops as a last resort, far preferring truck delivery, which they say would be possible to most of the country. The *Financial Times* reported that senior officials of NGOs were "scathing" and "scornful" in their reaction to the much-heralded U.S. air drop, dismissing it as a "propaganda ploy rather than a way to get aid to Afghans who really need help," a "propaganda tool" that was "exploiting humanitarian aid for cynical propaganda purposes" while the air strikes "had halted the only means of getting large volumes of food to Afghans—overland truck convoys" of the WFP ("UN concern as airstrikes bring relief effort to halt," "Relief workers hit at linking of food drops with air raids," *Financial Times*, October 9, citing Oxfam, Doctors without Borders, Christian Aid, Save the Children

Fund, and UN officials). Aid agencies were "scathingly critical about the nightly US airdrops." "They might as well just drop leaflets," a British aid worker commented, referring to the propaganda messages on the packages. "WFP officials say [air drops] would require workers on the ground to collect the food" and distribute it, and "must be made in daylight" and with adequate forewarning ("Scepticism grows over US food airdrops," *Financial Times*, October 10).

If these reactions are accurate, then the immediate effect of the bombing and the air drops of food that accompanied it was therefore to reduce significantly the food supplies available to the starving population, at least in the short term, while bringing the "nightmare scenario" a step closer. One can only hope that the torture will stop before the worst fears are realized, and that the suspension of desperately-needed food will be brief.

It is not easy to be optimistic about that, considering the attitudes expressed. For example, a *New York Times* report on an inside page casually mentions that "by the arithmetic of the United Nations, there will soon be 7.5 million Afghans in acute need of even a loaf of bread,...but with bombs falling," food deliveries by truck (the only significant contribution) have reduced by about half and there are only a few weeks before the harsh winter reduces the possibility of food distribution sharply (Barry Bearak, Oct. 15, B8). The further calculations are not given, but are not hard to carry out. Whatever happens, the fact that these appear to be the casual assumptions of planning and commentary defies comment.

NOAM CHOMSKY

We should also bear in mind that from the first days after the 9-11 attack, there has been nothing to stop massive food drops by air to the people imprisoned within the country that is once again being cruelly tortured; nor, apparently, the delivery of far greater quantities by truck, as the UN effort showed before it was suspended.

Whatever policies are adopted from this point on, a humanitarian catastrophe has already taken place, with worse to come. Perhaps the most apt description was given by the wonderful and courageous Indian writer and activist Arundhati Roy, referring to Operation Infinite Justice proclaimed by the Bush administration: "Witness the infinite justice of the new century. Civilians starving to death while they're waiting to be killed" (*Guardian*, September 29).

Her judgment loses no force from the fact that administration PR specialists realized that the phrase "infinite justice," suggesting the self-image of divinity, was another propaganda error, like "crusade." It was therefore changed to "enduring freedom"—in the light of the historical record, a phrase that defies comment.

The UN has indicated that the threat of starvation in Afghanistan is enormous. International criticism on this score has grown and now the U.S. and Britain are talking about providing food aid to ward off hunger. Are they caving in to dissent in fact, or only in appearance? What is their motivation? What will be the scale and impact of their efforts?

The United Nations estimates that some 7-8 million are at risk of imminent starvation. The *New York Times* reports in a small item (September 25) that nearly six million Afghans depend on food aid from the UN, as well as 3.5 million in refugee camps outside, many of whom fled just before the borders were sealed. The item reported that some food is being sent to the camps outside Afghanistan. Planners and commentators surely realize that they must do something to present themselves as humanitarians seeking to avert the awesome tragedy that unfolded at once after the threat of bombing and military attack, and the sealing of the borders they demanded. "Experts also urge the United States to improve its image by increasing aid to Afghan refugees, as well as by helping to rebuild the economy" (*Christian Science Monitor*, September 28). Even without PR specialists to instruct them, administration officials must comprehend that they should send some food to the refugees who made it across the border, and make at least some gesture towards providing food to starving people within: in order "to save lives" but also to "help the effort to find terror groups inside Afghanistan" (*Boston Globe*, September 27, quoting a Pentagon official, who describes this as "winning the hearts and minds of the people"). The *New York Times* editors picked up the same theme the following day, 12 days after the journal reported that the murderous operations were being put into effect.

On the scale of aid, one can only hope that it is enormous, or the human tragedy may be immense in a few weeks. If the government is sensible, there will be at least a show of the "massive air drops" that officials mention but have still not carried out as of September 30, not for lack of means.

International legal institutions would likely ratify efforts to arrest and try bin Laden and others, supposing guilt could be shown, including the use of force. Why does the U.S. avoid this recourse? Is it only a matter of not wishing to legitimate an approach that could be used, as well, against our acts of terrorism, or are other factors at play?

Much of the world has been asking the U.S. to provide some evidence to link bin Laden to the crime, and if such evidence could be provided, it would not be difficult to rally enormous support for an international effort, under the rubric of the UN, to apprehend and try him and his collaborators.

It's not impossible that this could be done through diplomatic means, as the Taliban have been indicating in various ways, though these moves are dismissed with contempt in favor of the use of force.

However, providing credible evidence is no simple matter. Even if bin Laden and his network are involved in the crimes of 9-11, it may be hard to produce credible evidence. And for all we know, most of the perpetrators may have killed themselves in their awful missions.

How hard it is to provide credible evidence was revealed

on October 5, when British Prime Minister Tony Blair proclaimed with great fanfare that there is now "absolutely no doubt" about the responsibility of bin Laden and the Taliban, releasing documentation based on what must be the most intensive investigative effort in history, combining the resources of all Western intelligence agencies and others. Despite the prima facie plausibility of the charge, and the unprecedented effort to establish it, the documentation is surprisingly thin. Only a small fraction of it even bears on the Sept. 11 crimes, and that little would surely not be taken seriously if presented as a charge against Western state criminals or their clients. The *Wall Street Journal* accurately described the documents as "more like a charge than detailed evidence," relegating the report to a back page. The *Journal* also points out, accurately, that it doesn't matter, quoting a senior U.S. official who says that "The criminal case is irrelevant. The plan is to wipe out Mr. bin Laden and his organization." The point of the documentation is to allow Blair, the Secretary General of NATO, and others to assure the world that the evidence is "clear and compelling."

It is highly unlikely that the case presented will be credible to people of the Middle East, as reported at once by Robert Fisk, or to others who look beyond headlines. Governments and their organizations, in contrast, have their own reasons to fall into line. One might ask why Washington's propaganda specialists chose to have Blair present the case: perhaps to sustain the image of holding back some highly convincing evidence for "security reasons," or in the hope that he would strike properly Churchillian poses.

In the background there are other minefields that planners must step through with care. To quote Arundhati Roy again, "The Taliban's response to U.S. demands for the extradition of bin Laden has been uncharacteristically reasonable: produce the evidence, then we'll hand him over. President Bush's response is that the demand is non-negotiable." She also adds one of the many reasons why this framework is unacceptable to Washington: "While talks are on for the extradition of CEOs, can India put in a side request for the extradition of Warren Anderson of the U.S.? He was the chairman of Union Carbide, responsible for the Bhopal gas leak that killed 16,000 people in 1984. We have collated the necessary evidence. It's all in the files. Could we have him, please?"

We needn't invent examples. The Haitian government has been asking the U.S. to extradite Emmanuel Constant, one of the most brutal of the paramilitary leaders while the (first) Bush and Clinton administrations (contrary to many illusions) were lending tacit support to the ruling junta and its rich constituency. Constant was tried in absentia in Haiti and sentenced to life in prison for his role in massacres. Has he been extradited? Does the matter evoke any detectable mainstream concern? To be sure, there are good reasons for the negative answers: extradition might lead to exposure of links that could be embarrassing in Washington. And after all, he was a leading figure in the slaughter of only about

5,000 people—relative to population, a few hundred thousand in the United States.

Such observations elicit frenzied tantrums at the extremist fringes of Western opinion, some of them called "the left." But for Westerners who have retained their sanity and moral integrity, and for many of the traditional victims, they are meaningful and instructive. Government leaders presumably understand that.

The single example that Roy mentions is only the beginning, of course; and it is one of the lesser examples, not only because of the scale of the atrocity, but because it was not explicitly a crime of state. Suppose Iran were to request the extradition of high officials of the Carter and Reagan administrations, refusing to present the ample evidence of the crimes they were implementing—and it surely exists. Or suppose Nicaragua were to demand the extradition of the newly-appointed ambassador to the UN, a man whose record includes his service as "proconsul" (as he was often called) in the virtual fiefdom of Honduras, where he surely was aware of the atrocities of the state terrorists he was supporting; and more significantly, includes his duties as local overseer of the terrorist war against Nicaragua, launched from Honduran bases. Would the U.S. agree to extradite them? Would the request even elicit ridicule?

That is only the barest beginning. The doors are better left closed, just as it is best to maintain the impressive silence that has reigned since the appointment of a leading figure in managing the operations condemned as terrorism

NOAM CHOMSKY

by the highest existing international bodies to lead a "war on terrorism." Even Jonathan Swift would be speechless.

That may be the reason why administration publicity experts preferred the ambiguous term "war" to the more explicit term "crime"—"crime against humanity" as Robert Fisk, Mary Robinson, and others have accurately depicted it.

If the Taliban regime falls and bin Laden or someone they claim is responsible is captured or killed, what next? What happens to Afghanistan? What happens more broadly in other regions?

The sensible administration plan would be to pursue the ongoing program of silent genocide, combined with humanitarian gestures to arouse the applause of the usual chorus who are called upon to sing the praises of the noble leaders who are dedicated to "principles and values" for the first time in history and are leading the world to a "new era" of idealism and commitment to "ending inhumanity" everywhere. Turkey is now very pleased to join Washington's "War against Terror," even to send ground troops. The reason, Prime Minister Ecevit said, is that Turkey owes the U.S. a special "debt of gratitude" because unlike European countries, Washington "had backed Ankara in its struggle against terrorism." He is referring to the 15-year war, peaking in the late 1990s with increasing U.S. aid, which left tens of thousands dead, 2-3 million refugees, and 3,500 towns and villages destroyed (seven times Kosovo under NATO bombs). Turkey was also lavishly praised and rewarded by Washington for joining the humanitarian effort in Kosovo, using the same U.S.-supplied F-16s that it had employed with such effectiveness in its own huge ethnic cleansing and state terror operations. The administration might also try to convert the Northern Alliance into a viable force, and may try to bring in other warlords hostile to it, like Washington's former favorite Gulbuddin Hekmatyar, now in Iran. Presumably British and U.S. commandos will undertake missions within Afghanistan, along with selective bombing, but scaled down so as not to recruit new forces for the cause of the radical Islamists.

U.S. campaigns should not be too casually compared to the failed Russian invasion of the 1980s. The Russians were facing a major army of perhaps 100,000 men or more, organized, trained, and heavily armed by the CIA and its associates. The U.S. is facing a ragtag force in a country that has already been virtually destroyed by 20 years of horror, for which we bear no slight share of responsibility. The Taliban forces, such as they are, might quickly collapse except for a small hardened core.

And one would expect that the surviving population would welcome an invading force if it is not too visibly associated with the murderous gangs that tore the country to shreds before the Taliban takeover. At this point, many people would be likely to welcome Genghis Khan.

What next? Expatriate Afghans and, apparently, some

NOAM CHOMSKY

internal elements who are not part of the Taliban inner circle have been calling for a UN effort to establish some kind of transition government, a process that might succeed in reconstructing something viable from the wreckage, if provided with very substantial reconstruction aid, channeled through independent sources like the UN or credible NGOs. That much should be the minimal responsibility of those who have turned this impoverished country into a land of terror, desperation, corpses, and mutilated victims. That could happen, but not without very substantial popular efforts in the rich and powerful societies. For the present, any such course has been ruled out by the Bush administration, which has announced that it will not be engaged in "nation building"—or, it seems so far (September 30), an effort that would be far more honorable and humane: substantial support, without interference, for "nation building" by others who might actually achieve some success in the enterprise. But current refusal to consider this decent course is not graven in stone.

What happens in other regions depends on internal factors, on the policies of foreign actors (the U.S. primary among them, for obvious reasons), and the way matters proceed in Afghanistan. One can say little with much confidence, but for many of the possible courses it is possible to make some reasonable assessments about the likely outcome—and there are a great many possibilities, too many to try to review in brief comments.

In order to shape an international alliance, the U.S. has suddenly shifted positions with a number of countries in the Middle East, Africa, and Asia, offering a variety of political, military and monetary packages in exchange for forms of support. How might these sudden moves be affecting the political dynamics in those regions?

Washington is stepping very delicately. We have to remember what is at stake: the world's major energy reserves, primarily in Saudi Arabia but throughout the Gulf region, along with not inconsiderable resources in Central Asia. Though a minor factor, Afghanistan has been discussed for years as a possible site for pipelines that will aid the U.S. in the complex maneuvering over control of Central Asian resources. North of Afghanistan, the states are fragile and violent. Uzbekistan is the most important. It has been condemned by Human Rights Watch for serious atrocities and is fighting its own internal Islamic insurgency. Tajikistan is similar, and is also a major drug-trafficking outlet to Europe, primarily in connection with the Northern Alliance, which controls much of the Afghan-Tajikistan border and has apparently been the major source of drugs since the Taliban virtually eliminated poppy production. Flight of Afghans to the north could lead to all sorts of internal problems. Pakistan, which has been the main supporter of the Taliban, has a strong internal radical Islamic movement. Its reaction is unpredictable, and potentially dangerous, if Pakistan is visibly used as a base for U.S. oper-

NOAM CHOMSKY

ations in Afghanistan; and there is much well-advised concern over the fact that Pakistan has nuclear weapons. The Pakistani military, while eager to obtain military aid from the U.S. (already promised), is wary, because of stormy past relations, and is also concerned over a potentially hostile Afghanistan allied with its enemy to the east, India. They are not pleased that the Northern Alliance is led by Tajiks, Uzbeks, and other Afghan minorities hostile to Pakistan and supported by India, Iran, and Russia, now the U.S. as well.

In the Gulf region, even wealthy and secular elements are bitter about U.S. policies and quietly often express support for bin Laden, whom they detest, as "the conscience of Islam" (*New York Times*, October 5, quoting an international lawyer for multinationals trained in the U.S.). Quietly, because these are highly repressive states; one factor in the general bitterness towards the U.S. is its support for these regimes. Internal conflict could easily spread, with consequences that could be enormous, especially if U.S. control over the huge resources of the region is threatened. Similar problems extend to North Africa and Southeast Asia, particularly Indonesia. Even apart from internal conflict, an increased flow of armaments to the countries of the region increases the likelihood of armed conflict and the flow of weapons to terrorist organizations and narcotraffickers. The governments are eager to join the U.S. "war against terrorism" to gain support for their own state terrorism, often on a shocking scale (Russia and Turkey, to mention only the most obvious examples, though Turkey has always benefited from crucial U.S. support).

Pakistan and India, border countries armed with nuclear weapons, have been eye to eye in serious conflict for years. How might the sudden and intense pressure that the U.S. is exerting in the region impact their already volatile relationship?

The main source of conflict is Kashmir, where India claims to be fighting Islamic terrorism, and Pakistan claims that India is refusing self-determination and has carried out large-scale terrorism itself. All the claims, unfortunately, are basically correct. There have been several wars over Kashmir, the latest one in 1999, when both states had nuclear weapons available; fortunately they were kept under control, but that can hardly be guaranteed. The threat of nuclear war is likely to increase if the U.S. persists in its militarization of space programs (euphemistically described as "missile defense"). These already include support for expansion of China's nuclear forces, in order to gain Chinese acquiescence to the programs. India will presumably try to match China's expansion, then Pakistan, then beyond, including Israel. Its nuclear capacities were described by the former head of the U.S. Strategic Command as "dangerous in the extreme," and one of the prime threats in the region.

"Volatile" is right, maybe worse.

Prior to 9-11, the Bush administration was being fiercely critiqued, ally nations included, for its political "unilateralism"—refusal to sign on to the Kyoto protocol for greenhouse emissions, intention to violate the ABM treaty in order to militarize space with a "missile defense" program, walkout of the racism conference in Durban, South Africa, to name only a few recent examples. Might the sudden U.S. alliance-building effort spawn a new "multilateralism" in which unexpected positive developments—like progress for Palestinians—might advance?

It's worth recalling that Bush's "unilateralism" was an extension of standard practice. In 1993, Clinton informed the UN that the U.S. will—as before—act "multilaterally when possible but unilaterally when necessary," and proceeded to do so. The position was reiterated by UN Ambassador Madeleine Albright and in 1999 by Secretary of Defense William Cohen, who declared that the U.S. is committed to "unilateral use of military power" to defend vital interests, which include "ensuring uninhibited access to key markets, energy supplies, and strategic resources," and indeed anything that Washington might determine to be within its own jurisdiction. But it is true that Bush went beyond, causing considerable anxiety among allies. The current need to form a coalition may attenuate the rhetoric but is unlikely to change the policies. Members of the coalition are expected to be silent and obedient supporters, not participants. The U.S. explicitly reserves to itself the right to act as it chooses, and is carefully avoiding any meaningful recourse to international institutions, as required by law. There are gestures to the contrary, but they lack any credibility, though governments will presumably accept them, bending to power, as they regularly do for their own reasons. The Palestinians are unlikely to gain anything. On the contrary, the terrorist attack of September 11 was a crushing blow to them, as they and Israel recognized immediately.

Since 9-11, Secretary of State Colin Powell has been signalling that the U.S. may adopt a new stance toward the plight of Palestinians. What is your reading?

My reading is exactly that of the officials and other sources quoted towards the end of the front-page story of the *New York Times*. They stressed that Bush-Powell do not even go as far as Clinton's Camp David proposals, lauded in the mainstream here but completely unacceptable, for reasons discussed accurately in Israel and elsewhere, and as anyone could see by looking at a map—one reason, I suppose, why maps were so hard to find here, though not elsewhere, including Israel. One can find more detail about this in articles at the time of Camp David, including my own, and essays in the collection edited by Roane Carey, *The New Intifada*.

The free flow of information is one of the first casualties of any war. Is the present situation in any way an exception? Examples?

NOAM CHOMSKY

Impediments to free flow of information in countries like the U.S. are rarely traceable to government; rather, to self-censorship of the familiar kind. The current situation is not exceptional—considerably better than the norm, in my opinion.

There are, however, some startling examples of U.S. government efforts to restrict free flow of information abroad. The Arab world has had one free and open news source, the satellite TV news channel Al-Jazeera in Qatar, modeled on BBC, with an enormous audience throughout the Arab-speaking world. It is the sole uncensored source, carrying a great deal of important news and also live debates and a wide range of opinion—broad enough to include Colin Powell a few days before 9-11 and Israeli Prime Minister Barak (me too, just to declare an interest). Al-Jazeera is also "the only international news organization to maintain reporters in the Taliban-controlled part of Afghanistan" (*Wall Street Journal*). Among other examples, it was responsible for the exclusive filming of the destruction of Buddhist statues that rightly infuriated the world. It has also provided lengthy interviews with bin Laden that I'm sure are perused closely by Western intelligence agencies and are invaluable to others who want to understand what he is thinking. These are translated and rebroadcast by BBC, several of them since 9-11.

Al-Jazeera is, naturally, despised and feared by the dictatorships of the region, particularly because of its frank exposures of their human rights records. The U.S. has joined their ranks. BBC reports that "The U.S. is not the first to feel aggrieved by Al-Jazeera coverage, which has in the past provoked anger from Algeria, Morocco, Saudi Arabia, Kuwait and Egypt for giving airtime to political dissidents."

The emir of Qatar confirmed that "Washington has asked Qatar to rein in the influential and editorially independent Arabic Al-Jazeera television station," BBC reported. The Emir, who also chairs the Organization of Islamic Conference that includes 56 countries, informed the press in Washington that Secretary of State Powell had pressured him to rein in Al-Jazeera: to "persuade Al-Jazeera to tone down its coverage," Al-Jazeera reports. Asked about the reports of censorship, the emir said: "This is true. We heard from the U.S. administration, and also from the previous U.S. administration" (BBC, October 4 citing Reuters).

The only serious report I noticed of this highly important news is in the *Wall Street Journal* (October 5), which also describes the reaction of intellectuals and scholars throughout the Arab world ("truly appalling," etc.). The report adds, as the Journal has done before, that "many Arab analysts argued that it is, after all, Washington's perceived disregard for human rights in officially pro-American countries such as Saudi Arabia that fuels the rampant anti-Americanism." There has also been remarkably little use of the bin Laden interviews and other material from Afghanistan available from Al-Jazeera.

After Al-Jazeera broadcast a tape of bin Laden that was highly useful to Western propaganda, and instantly received front-page coverage, the channel quickly became famous. The *New York Times* ran a story headlined "An Arab Station Offers Ground-Breaking Coverage" (Elaine Sciolino, October 9). The report lauded the channel as "the Arab world's CNN, with round-the-clock, all news and public affairs programs that reach millions of viewers." "The network has built a reputation for independent groundbreaking reporting that contrasts sharply with other Arab-language television stations," and "has focused on subjects considered subversive in most parts of the Arab world: the absence of democratic institutions, the persecution of political dissidents and the inequality of women." The story notes that "American policy makers have been troubled by Al Jazeera's" broadcasts of bin Laden interviews and the "anti-American oratory" of analysts, guests, and "callers on freewheeling phone-in shows." The rest is unmentioned, though there was a mild editorial admonition the next day.

So yes, there are barriers to free flow of information, but they cannot be blamed on government censorship or pressure, a very marginal factor in the United States.

What do you believe should be the role and priority of social activists concerned about justice at this time? Should we curb our criticisms, as some have claimed, or is this, instead, a time for renewed and enlarged efforts, not only because it is a crisis regarding which we can attempt to have a very important positive impact, but also because large sectors of the public are actually far more receptive than usual to discussion and exploration, even if other sectors are intransigently hostile?

It depends on what these social activists are trying to achieve. If their goal is to escalate the cycle of violence and to increase the likelihood of further atrocities like that of September 11—and, regrettably, even worse ones with which much of the world is all too familiar—then they should certainly curb their analysis and criticisms, refuse to think, and cut back their involvement in the very serious issues in which they have been engaged. The same advice is warranted if they want to help the most reactionary and regressive elements of the political-economic power system to implement plans that will be of great harm to the general population here and in much of the world, and may even threaten human survival. If, on the contrary, the goal of social activists is to reduce the likelihood of further atrocities, and to advance hopes for freedom, human rights, and democracy, then they should follow the opposite course. They should intensify their efforts to inquire into the background factors that lie behind these and other crimes and devote themselves with even more energy to the just causes to which they have already been committed. They should listen when the bishop of the southern Mexican city of San Cristobal de las Casas, who has seen his share of misery and oppression, urges Northamericans to "reflect on why they are so hated" after the U.S. "has generated so much violence to protect its economic interests" (Marion Lloyd, Mexico City, *Boston Globe*, September 30).

NOAM CHOMSKY

It is surely more comforting to listen to the words of liberal commentators who assure us that "They hate us because we champion a 'new world order' of capitalism, individualism, secularism and democracy that should be the norm everywhere" (Ronald Steel, *New York Times*, September 14). Or Anthony Lewis, who assures us that the only relevance of our past policies is that they "negatively affect public attitudes in the Arab world toward the coalition's antiterrorism effort" (*New York Times*, October 6). What we have done, he declares confidently, can have had no effect on the goals of the terrorists. What they say is so utterly irrelevant that it can be ignored, and we can also dismiss the conformity between what they have been saying and their specific actions for 20 years of terror—hardly obscure, and reported extensively by serious journalists and scholars. It is a necessary truth, requiring no evidence or argument, that the terrorists seek "the violent transformation of an irremediably sinful and unjust world" and stand only for "apocalyptic nihilism" (quoting Michael Ignatieff with approval). Neither their professed goals and actions nor the clearly articulated attitudes of the population of the region—even highly pro-American Kuwaitis—make the slightest bit of difference. We must therefore disregard anything we have done that might provoke such responses.

More comforting, no doubt, but not more wise, if we care about what lies ahead.

The opportunities are surely there. The shock of the horrendous crimes has already opened elite sectors to reflection of a kind that would have been hard to imagine not long ago, and among the general public that is even more true. Just to speak about personal experience, aside from near-constant interviews with national radio-TV-press in Europe and elsewhere, I have had considerably more access even to mainstream media in the U.S. than ever before, and others report the same experience.

Of course, there will be those who demand silent obedience. We expect that from the ultra-right, and anyone with a little familiarity with history will expect it from some left intellectuals as well, perhaps in an even more virulent form. But it is important not to be intimidated by hysterical ranting and lies and to keep as closely as one can to the course of truth and honesty and concern for the human consequences of what one does, or fails to do. All truisms, but worth bearing in mind.

Beyond the truisms, we turn to specific questions, for inquiry and for action.

APPENDIX A

DEPARTMENT OF STATE
Report on Foreign Terrorist Organizations
Released by the Office of the Coordinator for
Counterterrorism
October 5, 2001

BACKGROUND

The Secretary of State designates Foreign Terrorist Organizations (FTO's), in consultation with the Attorney General and the Secretary of the Treasury. These designations are undertaken pursuant to the Immigration and Nationality Act, as amended by the Antiterrorism and Effective Death Penalty Act of 1996. FTO designations are valid for two years, after which they must be redesignated or they automatically expire. Redesignation after two years is a positive act and represents a determination by the Secretary of State that the organization has continued to engage in terrorist activity and still meets the criteria specified in law.

In October 1997, former Secretary of State Madeleine K. Albright approved the designation of the first 30 groups as Foreign Terrorist Organizations.

In October 1999, Secretary Albright re-certified 27 of these groups' designations but allowed three organizations to drop from the list because their involvement in terrorist activity had ended and they no longer met the criteria for designation.

Secretary Albright designated one new FTO in 1999 (al Qa'ida) and another in 2000 (Islamic Movement of Uzbekistan).

Secretary of State Colin L. Powell has designated two new FTO's (Real IRA and AUC) in 2001.

In October 2001, Secretary Powell re-certified the designation of 26 of the 28 FTO's whose designation was due to expire, and combined two previously designated groups (Kahane Chai and Kach) into one.

Current List of Designated Foreign Terrorist Organizations (as of October 5, 2001):

1. Abu Nidal Organization (ANO)
2. Abu Sayyaf Group
3. Armed Islamic Group (GIA)
4. Aum Shinrikyo
5. Basque Fatherland and Liberty (ETA)
6. Gama'a al-Islamiyya (Islamic Group)
7. HAMAS (Islamic Resistance Movement)
8. Harakat ul-Mujahidin (HUM)
9. Hizballah (Party of God)
10. Islamic Movement of Uzbekistan (IMU)
11. al-Jihad (Egyptian Islamic Jihad)
12. Kahane Chai (Kach)
13. Kurdistan Workers' Party (PKK)
14. Liberation Tigers of Tamil Eelam (LTTE)
15. Mujahedin-e Khalq Organization (MEK)
16. National Liberation Army (ELN)
17. Palestinian Islamic Jihad (PIJ)
18. Palestine Liberation Front (PLF)
19. Popular Front for the Liberation of Palestine (PFLP)

NOAM CHOMSKY

20. PFLP-General Command (PFLP-GC)
21. al-Qa'ida
22. Real IRA
23. Revolutionary Armed Forces of Colombia (FARC)
24. Revolutionary Nuclei (formerly ELA)
25. Revolutionary Organization 17 November
26. Revolutionary People's Liberation Army/Front (DHKP/C)
27. Shining Path (Sendero Luminoso, SL)
28. United Self-Defense Forces of Colombia (AUC)

NOTE: For descriptions of these foreign terrorist organizations, please refer to "Patterns of Global Terrorism: 2000."

LEGAL CRITERIA FOR DESIGNATION

1. The organization must be foreign.

2. The organization must engage in terrorist activity as defined in Section 212 (a)(3)(B) of the Immigration and Nationality Act.* (see below)

3. The organization's activities must threaten the security of U.S. nationals or the national security (national defense, foreign relations, or the economic interests) of the United States.

EFFECTS OF DESIGNATION

LEGAL

1. It is unlawful for a person in the United States or subject to the jurisdiction of the United States to provide funds or other material support to a designated FTO.

2. Representatives and certain members of a designated FTO, if they are aliens, can be denied visas or excluded from the United States.

3. U.S. financial institutions must block funds of designated FTO's and their agents and report the blockage to the Office of Foreign Assets Control, U.S. Department of the Treasury.

OTHER EFFECTS
1. Deters donations or contributions to named organizations
2. Heightens public awareness and knowledge of terrorist organizations
3. Signals to other governments our concern about named organizations
4. Stigmatizes and isolates designated terrorist organizations internationally

THE PROCESS

The Secretary of State makes decisions concerning the designation and redesignation of FTO's following an exhaustive interagency review process in which all evidence of a group's activity, from both classified and open sources, is scrutinized. The State Department, working closely with the Justice and Treasury Departments and the intelligence community, prepares a detailed "administrative record" which documents the terrorist activity of the designated FTO. Seven days before publishing an FTO designation in the Federal Register, the Department of State provides classified notification to Congress.

Under the statute, designations are subject to judicial review. In the event of a challenge to a group's FTO designation in federal court, the U.S. government relies upon the administrative record to defend the Secretary's decision. These administrative records contain intelligence information and are therefore classified.

FTO designations expire in two years unless renewed. The

NOAM CHOMSKY

law allows groups to be added at any time following a decision by the Secretary, in consultation with the Attorney General and the Secretary of the Treasury. The Secretary may also revoke designations after determining that there are grounds for doing so and notifying Congress.

* The Immigration and Nationality Act defines terrorist activity to mean: any activity which is unlawful under the laws of the place where it is committed (or which, if committed in the United States, would be unlawful under the laws of the United States or any State) and which involves any of the following:

(I) The highjacking or sabotage of any conveyance (including an aircraft, vessel, or vehicle).

(II) The seizing or detaining, and threatening to kill, injure, or continue to detain, another individual in order to compel a third person (including a governmental organization) to do or abstain from doing any act as an explicit or implicit condition for the release of the individual seized or detained.

(III) A violent attack upon an internationally protected person (as defined in section 1116(b)(4) of title 18, United States Code) or upon the liberty of such a person.

(IV) An assassination.

(V) The use of any—
   (a) biological agent, chemical agent, or nuclear weapon or device, or
   (b) explosive or firearm (other than for mere personal mone-

tary gain), with intent to endanger, directly or indirectly, the safety of one or more individuals or to cause substantial damage to property.

(VI) A threat, attempt, or conspiracy to do any of the foregoing.

(iii) The term "engage in terrorist activity" means to commit, in an individual capacity or as a member of an organization, an act of terrorist activity or an act which the actor knows, or reasonably should know, affords material support to any individual, organization, or government in conducting a terrorist activity at any time, including any of the following acts:

(I) The preparation or planning of a terrorist activity.

(II) The gathering of information on potential targets for terrorist activity.

(III) The providing of any type of material support, including a safe house, transportation, communications, funds, false documentation or identification, weapons, explosives, or training, to any individual the actor knows or has reason to believe has committed or plans to commit a terrorist activity.

(IV) The soliciting of funds or other things of value for terrorist activity or for any terrorist organization.

(V) The solicitation of any individual for membership in a terrorist organization, terrorist government, or to engage in a terrorist activity.

NOAM CHOMSKY

APPENDIX B

RECOMMENDED READING

Noam Chomsky, *Culture of Terrorism* (South End Press, 1988).

Noam Chomsky, *Necessary Illusions* (South End Press, 1989).

Noam Chomsky, *Pirates and Emperors* (Claremont, 1986; reprinted by Amana, Black Rose, Pluto).

Chomsky and E.S. Herman, *Political Economy of Human Rights* (South End Press, 1979).

John Cooley, *Unholy Wars: Afghanistan, America and International Terrorism* (Pluto, 1999, 2001).

Alex George, ed., *Western State Terrorism* (Polity-Blackwell, 1991).

Herman, *Real Terror Network* (South End Press, 1982).

Herman and Chomsky, *Manufacturing Consent* (Pantheon, 1998, 2001).

Herman and Gerry O'Sullivan, *The 'Terrorism' Industry* (Pantheon, 1990).

Walter Laqueur, *Age of Terrorism* (Little, Brown and Co., 1987).

Michael McClintock, *Instruments of Statecraft* (Pantheon, 1992).

Paul Wilkinson, *Terrorism and the Liberal State* (NYU Press, 1986).

MEDIA CONTROL

THE SPECTACULAR
ACHIEVEMENTS OF PROPAGANDA

SECOND EDITION

NOAM CHOMSKY

CONTENTS

THE ROLE OF THE MEDIA in contemporary politics forces us to ask what kind of a world and what kind of a society we want to live in, and in particular in what sense of democracy do we want this to be a democratic society? Let me begin by counter-posing two different conceptions of democracy. One conception of democracy has it that a democratic society is one in which the public has the means to participate in some meaningful way in the management of their own affairs and the means of information are open and free. If you look up democracy in the dictionary you'll get a definition something like that.

An alternative conception of democracy is that the public must be barred from managing of their own affairs and the means of information must be kept narrowly and rigidly controlled. That may sound like an odd conception of democracy, but it's important to understand that it is the prevailing conception. In fact, it has long been, not just in operation, but even in theory. There's a long history that goes back to the earliest modern democratic revolutions in seventeenth century England which largely expresses this point of view. I'm just going to keep to the modern period and say a few words about how that notion of democracy develops and why and how the problem of media and disinformation enters within that context.

Let's begin with the first modern government propaganda operation. That was under the Woodrow Wilson Administration. Woodrow Wilson was elected President in 1916 on the platform "Peace Without Victory." That was right in the middle of the World War I. The population was extremely pacifistic and saw no reason to become involved in a European war. The Wilson administration was actually committed to war and had to do something about it. They established a government propaganda commission, called the Creel Commission, which succeeded, within six months, in turning a pacifist population into a hysterical, war–mongering popu-

11

lation which wanted to destroy everything German, tear the Germans limb from limb, go to war and save the world. That was a major achievement, and it led to a further achievement. Right at that time and after the war the same techniques were used to whip up a hysterical Red Scare, as it was called, which succeeded pretty much in destroying unions and eliminating such dangerous problems as freedom of the press and freedom of political thought. There was very strong support from the media, from the business establishment, which in fact organized, pushed much of this work, and it was, in general, a great success.

Among those who participated actively and enthusiastically in Wilson's war were the progressive intellectuals, people of the John Dewey circle, who took great pride, as you can see from their own writings at the time, in having shown that what they called the "more intelligent members of the community," namely, themselves, were able to drive a reluctant population into a war by terrifying them and eliciting jingoist fanaticism. The means that were used were extensive. For example, there was a good deal of fabrication of atrocities by the Huns, Belgian babies with their arms torn off, all sorts of awful things that you still read in history books. Much of it was invented by the British propaganda ministry, whose own commitment at the time, as they put it in their secret deliberations, was "to direct the thought of most of the world." But more crucially they wanted to control the thought of the more intelligent members of the community in the United States, who would then disseminate the propaganda that they were concocting and convert the pacifistic country to wartime hysteria. That worked. It worked very well. And it taught a lesson: State propaganda, when supported by the educated classes and when no deviation is permitted from it, can have a big effect. It was a lesson learned by Hitler and many others, and it has been pursued to this day.

SPECTATOR DEMOCRACY

Another group that was impressed by these successes was liberal democratic theorists and leading media figures, like, for example, Walter Lippmann, who was the dean of American journalists, a major foreign and domestic policy critic and also a major theorist of liberal democracy. If you take a look at his collected essays, you'll see that they're subtitled something like "A Progressive Theory of Liberal Democratic Thought." Lippmann was involved in these propaganda commissions and recognized their achievements. He argued that what he called a "revolution in the art of democracy," could be used to "manufacture consent, " that is, to bring about agreement on the part of the public for things that they didn't want by the new techniques of propaganda. He also thought that this was a good idea, in fact, necessary. It was necessary because, as he put it, "the common interests elude public opinion entirely" and can only be understood and managed by a "specialized class "of "responsible men" who are smart enough to figure things out. This theory asserts that only a small elite, the intellectual community that the Deweyites were talking about, can understand the common interests, what all of us care about, and that these things "elude the general public." This is a view that goes back hundreds of years. It's also a typical Leninist view. In fact, it has very close resemblance to the Leninist conception that a vanguard of revolutionary intellectuals take state power, using popular revolutions as the force that brings them to state power, and then drive the stupid masses toward a future that they're too dumb and incompetent to envision for themselves. The liberal democratic theory and Marxism–Leninism are very close in their common ideological assumptions. I think that's one reason why people have found it so easy over the years to drift from one position to another without any particular sense of change. It's just a matter of assessing where power is. Maybe there will be a popular revolution, and that will put us into state power; or maybe there won't be, in which case we'll just work for the people with real power: the business community. But we'll do the same thing. We'll drive the stupid masses toward a world that they're too dumb to understand for themselves.

Lippmann backed this up by a pretty elaborated theory of progressive democracy. He argued that in a properly functioning democracy there are classes of citizens. There is first of all the class of citizens who have to take some active role in running general affairs. That's the specialized class. They are the people who analyze, execute, make decisions, and run things in the political, economic, and ideological systems. That's a small percentage of the population. Naturally, anyone who puts these ideas forth is always part of that small group, and they're talking about what to do about *those others*. Those others, who are out of the small group, the big majority of the population, they are what Lippmann called "the bewildered herd." We have to protect ourselves from "the trampling and roar of a bewildered herd". Now there are two "functions" in a democracy: The specialized class, the responsible men, carry out the executive function, which means they do the thinking and planning and understand the common interests. Then, there is the bewildered herd, and they have a function in democracy too. Their function in a democracy, he said, is to be "spectators," not participants in action. But they have more of a function than that, because it's a democracy. Occasionally they are allowed to lend their weight to one or another member of the specialized class. In other words, they're allowed to say, "We want you to be our leader" or "We want *you* to be our leader." That's because it's a democracy and not a totalitarian state. That's called an election. But once they've lent their weight to one or another member of the specialized class they're supposed to sink back and become spectators of action, but not participants. That's in a properly functioning democracy.

And there's a logic behind it. There's even a kind of compelling moral principle behind it. The compelling moral principle is that the mass of the public are just too stupid to be able to understand things. If they try to participate in managing their own affairs, they're just going to cause trouble. Therefore, it would be immoral and improper to permit them to do this. We have to tame the bewildered herd, not allow the bewildered herd to rage and trample and destroy things. It's pretty much the same logic that says that it would be improper to let a three-year-old run across the street. You don't give a three-year-old that kind of freedom because the three-year-old doesn't know how to handle that freedom. Correspondingly, you don't allow the bewildered herd to become participants in action. They'll just cause trouble.

So we need something to tame the bewildered herd, and that something is this new revolution in the art of democracy: the manufacture of consent. The media, the schools, and popular culture have to be divided. For the political class and the decision makers they have to provide them some tolerable sense of reality, although they also have to instill the proper beliefs. Just remember, there is an unstated premise here. The unstated premise —and even the responsible men have to disguise this from themselves—has to do with the question of how they get into the position where they have the authority to make decisions. The way they do that, of course, is by serving people with *real* power. The people with real power are the ones who own the society, which is a pretty narrow group. If the specialized class can come along and say, I can serve your interests, then they'll be part of the executive group. You've got to keep that quiet. That means they have to have instilled in them the beliefs and doctrines that will serve the interests of private power. Unless they can master that skill, they're not part of the specialized class. So we have one kind of educational system directed to the responsible men, the specialized class. They have to be deeply indoctrinated in the values and interests of private power and the state-corporate nexus that represents it. If they can achieve that, then they can be part of the specialized class. The rest of the bewildered herd basically just have to be distracted. Turn their attention to something else. Keep them out of trouble. Make sure that they remain at most spectators of action, occasionally lending their weight to one or another of the real leaders, who they may select among.

This point of view has been developed by lots of other people. In fact, it's pretty conventional. For example, the leading theologian and foreign policy critic Reinhold Niebuhr, sometimes called "the theologian of the establishment," the guru of George Kennan and the Kennedy intellectuals, put it that rationality is a very narrowly restricted skill. Only a small number of people have it. Most people are guided by just emotion and impulse. Those of us who have rationality have to create "necessary illusions" and emotionally potent "oversimplifications" to keep the naïve simpletons more or less on course. This became a substantial part of contemporary political science. In the 1920s and early 1930s, Harold Lasswell, the founder of the modern field of communications and one of the leading American political scientists, explained that we should not succumb to "democratic dogmatisms about men being the best judges of their own interests." Because they're not. We're the best judges of the public interests. Therefore, just out of ordinary morality, we have to make sure that they don't have an opportunity to act on the basis of their misjudgments. In what is nowadays called a totalitarian state, or a military state, it's easy. You just hold a bludgeon over their heads, and if they get out of line you smash them over the head. But as society has become more free and democratic, you lose that capacity. Therefore you have to turn to the techniques of propaganda. The logic is clear. Propaganda is to a democracy what the bludgeon is to a totalitarian state. That's wise and good because, again, the common interests elude the bewildered herd. They can't figure them out.

The United States pioneered the public relations industry. Its commitment was "to control the public mind," as its leaders put it. They learned a lot from the successes of the Creel Commission and the successes in creating the Red Scare and its aftermath. The public relations industry underwent a huge expansion at that time. It succeeded for some time in creating almost total subordination of the public to business rule through the 1920s. This was so extreme that Congressional committees began to investigate it as we moved into the 1930s. That's where a lot of our information about it comes from.

Public relations is a huge industry. They're spending by now something on the order of a billion dollars a year. All along its commitment was to *controlling the public mind*. In the 1930s, big problems arose again, as they had during the First World War. There was a huge depression and substantial labor organizing. In fact, in 1935 labor won its first major legislative victory, namely, the right to organize, with the Wagner Act. That raised two serious problems. For one thing, democracy was misfunctioning. The bewildered herd was actually winning legislative victories, and it's not supposed to work that way. The other problem was that it was becoming possible for people to organize. People have to be atomized and segregated and alone. They're not supposed to organize, because then they might be something beyond spectators of action. They might actually be participants if many people with limited resources could get together to enter the political arena. That's really threatening. A major response was taken on the part of business to ensure that this would be the last legislative victory for labor and that it would be the beginning of the end of this democratic deviation of popular organization. It worked. That was the last legislative victory for labor. From that point on—although the number of people in the unions increased for a while during the World War II, after which it started dropping—the capacity to act through the unions began to steadily drop. It wasn't by accident. We're now talking about the business community, which spends lots and lots of money, attention, and thought into how to deal with these problems through the public relations industry and other organizations, like the National Association of Manufacturers and the Business Roundtable, and so on. They immediately set to work to try to find a way to counter these democratic deviations.

The first trial was one year later, in 1937. There was a major strike, the Steel strike in western Pennsylvania at Johnstown. Business tried out a new technique of labor destruction, which worked very well. Not through goon squads and breaking knees. That wasn't working very well any more, but through the more subtle and effective means of propaganda. The idea was to figure out ways to turn the public against the strikers, to present the strikers as disruptive, harmful to the public and against the common interests. The common interests are those of "us," the businessman, the worker, the housewife. That's all "us." We want to be together and have things like harmony and Americanism and working together. Then there's those bad strikers out there who are disruptive and causing trouble and breaking harmony and violating Americanism. We've got to stop them so we can all live together. The corporate executive and the guy who cleans the floors all have the same interests. We can all work together and work for Americanism in harmony, liking each other. That was essentially the message. A huge amount of effort was put into presenting it. This is, after all, the business community, so they control the media and have massive resources. And it worked, very effectively. It was later called the "Mohawk Valley formula" and applied over and over again to break strikes. They were called "scientific methods of strike-breaking," and worked very effectively by mobilizing community opinion in favor of vapid, empty concepts like Americanism. Who can be against that? Or harmony. Who can be against that? Or, as in the Persian Gulf War, "Support our troops." Who can be against that? Or yellow ribbons. Who can be against that? Anything that's totally vacuous.

In fact, what does it mean if somebody asks you, Do you support the people in Iowa? Can you say, Yes, I support them, or No, I don't support them? It's not even a question. It doesn't mean anything.

That's the point. The point of public relations slogans like "Support our troops" is that they don't mean anything. They mean as much as whether you support the people in Iowa. Of course, there was an issue. The issue was, Do you support our policy? But you don't want people to think about that issue. That's the whole point of good propaganda. You want to create a slogan that nobody's going to be against, and everybody's going to be for. Nobody knows what it means, because it doesn't mean anything. Its crucial value is that it diverts your attention from a question that *does* mean something: Do you support our policy? That's the one you're not allowed to talk about. So you have people arguing about support for the troops? "Of course I don't *not* support them." Then you've won. That's like Americanism and harmony. We're all together, empty slogans, let's join in, let's make sure we don't have these bad people around to disrupt our harmony with their talk about class struggle, rights and that sort of business.

That's all very effective. It runs right up to today. And of course it is carefully thought out. The people in the public relations industry aren't there for the fun of it. They're doing work. They're trying to instill the right values. In fact, they have a conception of what democracy ought to be: It ought to be a system in which the specialized class is trained to work in the service of the masters, the people who own the society. The rest of the population ought to be deprived of any form of organization, because organization just causes trouble. They ought to be sitting alone in front of the TV and having drilled into their heads the message, which says, the only value in life is to have more commodities or live like that rich middle class family you're watching and to have nice values like harmony and Americanism. That's all there is in life. You may think in your own head that there's got to be something more in life than this, but since you're watching the tube alone you assume, I must be crazy, because that's all that's going on over there. And since there is no organization permitted—that's absolutely crucial—you never have a way of finding out whether you are crazy, and you just assume it, because it's the natural thing to assume.

So that's the ideal. Great efforts are made in trying to achieve that ideal. Obviously, there is a certain conception behind it. The conception of democracy is the one that I mentioned. The bewildered herd is a problem. We've got to prevent their roar and trampling. We've got to distract them. They should be watching the Superbowl or sitcoms or violent movies. Every once in a while you call on them to chant meaningless slogans like "Support our troops." You've got to keep them pretty scared, because unless they're properly scared and frightened of all kinds of devils that are going to destroy them from outside or inside or somewhere, they may start to think, which is very dangerous, because they're not competent to think. Therefore it's important to distract them and marginalize them.

That's one conception of democracy. In fact, going back to the business community, the last legal victory for labor really was 1935, the Wagner Act. After the war came, the unions declined as did a very rich working class culture that was associated with the unions. That was destroyed. We moved to a business–run society at a remarkable level. This is the only state-capitalist industrial society which doesn't have even the normal social contract that you find in comparable societies. Outside of South Africa, I guess, this is the only industrial society that doesn't have national health care. There's no general commitment to even minimal standards of survival for the parts of the population who can't follow those rules and gain things for themselves individually. Unions are virtually nonexistent. Other forms of popular structure are virtually nonexistent. There are no political parties or organizations. It's a long way toward the ideal, at least structurally. The media are a corporate monopoly. They have the same point of view. The two parties are two factions of the business party. Most of the population doesn't even bother voting because it looks meaningless. They're marginalized and properly distracted. At least that's the goal. The leading figure in the public relations industry, Edward Bernays, actually came out of the Creel Commission. He was part of it, learned his lessons there and went on to develop what he called the "engineering of consent," which he described as "the essence of democracy." The people who are able to engineer consent are the ones who have the resources and the power to do it—the business community—and that's who you work for.

ENGINEERING OPINION

It is also necessary to whip up the population in support of foreign adventures. Usually the population is pacifist, just like they were during the First World War. The public sees no reason to get involved in foreign adventures, killing, and torture. So you *have* to whip them up. And to whip them up you have to frighten them. Bernays himself had an important achievement in this respect. He was the person who ran the public relations campaign for the United Fruit Company in 1954, when the United States moved in to overthrow the capitalist-democratic government of Guatemala and installed a murderous death-squad society, which remains that way to the present day with constant infusions of U.S. aid to prevent in more than empty form democratic deviations. It's necessary to constantly ram through domestic programs which the public is opposed to, because there is no reason for the public to be in favor of domestic programs that are harmful to them. *This*, too, takes extensive propaganda. We've seen a lot of this in the last ten years. The Reagan programs were overwhelmingly unpopular. Voters in the 1984 "Reagan landslide," by about three to two, hoped that his policies would not be enacted. If you take particular programs, like armaments, cutting back on social spending, etc., almost every one of them was overwhelmingly opposed by the public. But as long as people are marginalized and distracted and have no way to organize or articulate their sentiments, or even know that others have these sentiments, people who said that they prefer social spending to military spending, who gave that answer on polls, as people overwhelmingly did, assumed that they were the only people with that crazy idea in their heads. They never heard it from anywhere else. Nobody's supposed to think that. Therefore, if you do think it and you answer it in a poll, you just assume that you're sort of weird. Since there's no way to get together with other people who share or reinforce that view and help you articulate it, you feel like an oddity, an oddball. So you just stay on the side and you don't pay any attention to what's going on. You look at something else, like the Superbowl.

To a certain extent, then, that ideal was achieved, but never completely. There are institutions which it has as yet been impossible to destroy. The churches, for example, still exist. A large part of the dissident activity in the United States comes out of the churches, for the simple reason that they're there. So when you go to a European country and give a political talk, it may very likely be in the union hall. Here that won't happen, because unions first of all barely exist, and if they do exist they're not political organizations. But the churches do exist, and therefore you often give a talk in a church. Central American solidarity work mostly grew out of the churches, mainly because they exist.

The bewildered herd never gets properly tamed, so this is a constant battle. In the 1930s they arose again and were put down. In the 1960s there was another wave of dissidence. There was a name for that. It was called by the specialized class "the crisis of democracy." Democracy was regarded as entering into a crisis in the 1960s. The crisis was that large segments of the population were becoming organized and active and trying to participate in the political arena. Here we come back to these two conceptions of democracy. By the dictionary definition, that's an *advance* in democracy. By the prevailing conception that's a *problem*, a crisis that has to be overcome. The population has to be driven back to the apathy, obedience and passivity that is their proper state. We therefore have to do something to overcome the crisis. Efforts were made to achieve that. It hasn't worked. The crisis of democracy is still alive and well, fortunately, but not very effective in changing policy. But it is effective in changing opinion, contrary to what a lot of people believe. Great efforts were made after the 1960s to try to reverse and overcome this malady. One aspect of the malady actually got a technical name. It was called the "Vietnam Syndrome." The Vietnam Syndrome, a term that began to come up around 1970, has actually been defined on occasion. The Reaganite intellectual Norman Podhoretz defined it as "the sickly inhibitions against the use of military force." There were these sickly inhibitions against violence on the part of a large part of the public.

People just didn't understand why we should go around torturing people and killing people and carpet bombing them. It's very dangerous for a population to be overcome by these sickly inhibitions, as Goebbels understood, because then there's a limit on foreign adventures. It's necessary, as the *Washington Post* put it rather proudly during the Gulf War hysteria, to instill in people respect for "martial value." That's important. If you want to have a violent society that uses force around the world to achieve the ends of its own domestic elite, it's necessary to have a proper appreciation of the martial virtues and none of these sickly inhibitions about using violence. So that's the Vietnam Syndrome. It's necessary to overcome that one.

REPRESENTATION AS REALITY

It's also necessary to completely falsify history. That's another way to overcome these sickly inhibitions, to make it look as if when we attack and destroy somebody we're really protecting and defending ourselves against major aggressors and monsters and so on. There has been a *huge* effort since the Vietnam war to reconstruct the history of that. Too many people began to understand what was really going on. Including plenty of soldiers and a lot of young people who were involved with the peace movement and others. That was bad. It was necessary to rearrange those bad thoughts and to restore some form of sanity, namely, a recognition that whatever we do is noble and right. If we're bombing South

35

Vietnam, that's because we're defending South Vietnam against somebody, namely, the South Vietnamese, since nobody else was there. It's what the Kennedy intellectuals called defense against "internal aggression" in South Vietnam. That was the phrase used by Adlai Stevenson and others. It was necessary to make that the official and well understood picture. That's worked pretty well. When you have total control over the media and the educational system and scholarship is conformist, you can get that across. One indication of it was revealed in a study done at the University of Massachusetts on attitudes toward the current Gulf crisis—a study of beliefs and attitudes in television watching. One of the questions asked in that study was, How many Vietnamese casualties would you estimate that there were during the Vietnam war? The average response on the part of Americans today is about 100,000. The official figure is about two million. The actual figure is probably three to four million. The people who conducted the study raised an appropriate question: What would we think about German political culture if, when you asked people today how many Jews died in the Holocaust, they estimated about 300,000? What would that tell us about German political culture? They leave the question unanswered, but you can pursue it. What does it tell us about our culture? It tells us quite a bit. It is necessary to overcome the sickly inhibitions against the use of military force and other democratic deviations. In this particular case it worked. This is true on every topic. Pick the topic you like: the Middle East, international terrorism, Central America, whatever it is—the picture of the world that's presented to the public has only the remotest relation to reality. The truth of the matter is buried under edifice after edifice of lies upon lies. It's all been a marvelous success from the point of view in deterring the threat of democracy, achieved under conditions of freedom, which is extremely interesting. It's not like a totalitarian state, where it's done by force. These achievements are under conditions of freedom. If we want to understand our own society, we'll have to think about these facts. They are important facts, important for those who care about what kind of society they live in.

DISSIDENT CULTURE

Despite all of this, the dissident culture survived. It's grown quite a lot since the 1960s. In the 1960s the dissident culture first of all was extremely slow in developing. There was no protest against the Indochina war until years after the United States had started bombing South Vietnam. When it did grow it was a very narrow dissident movement, mostly students and young people. By the 1970s that had changed considerably. Major popular movements had developed: the environmental movement, the feminist movement, the anti-nuclear movement, and others. In the 1980s there was an even greater expansion to the solidarity movements, which is something very new and important in the history of at least American, and maybe even world dissidence. These were movements that not only protested but actually involved themselves, often intimately, in the lives of suffering people elsewhere. They learned a great deal from it and had quite a civilizing effect on mainstream America. All of this has made a very large difference. Anyone who has been involved in this kind of activity for many years must be aware of this. I know myself that the kind of talks I give today in the most reactionary parts of the country—central Georgia, rural Kentucky, etc.—are talks of the kind that I couldn't have given at the peak of the peace movement to the most active peace movement audience. Now you can give them anywhere. People may agree or not agree, but at least they understand what you're talking about and there's some sort of common ground that you can pursue.

These are all signs of the civilizing effect, despite all the propaganda, despite all the efforts to control thought and manufacture consent. Nevertheless, people are acquiring an ability and a willingness to think things through. Skepticism about power has grown, and attitudes have changed on many, many issues. It's kind of slow, maybe even glacial, but perceptible and important. Whether it's fast enough to make a significant difference in what happens in the world is another question. Just to take one familiar example of it: The famous gender gap. In the 1960s attitudes of men and women were approximately the same on such matters as the "martial virtues" and the sickly inhibitions against the use of military force. Nobody, neither men nor women, were suffering from those sickly inhibitions in the early 1960s. The responses were the same. Everybody thought that the use of violence to suppress people out there was just right. Over the years it's changed. The sickly inhibitions have increased all across the board. But meanwhile a gap has been growing, and by now it's a very substantial gap. According to polls, it's something like twenty-five percent. What has happened? What has happened is that there is some form of at least semi-organized popular movement that women are involved in—the feminist movement. Organization has its effects. It means that you discover that you're not alone. Others have the same thoughts that you do. You can reinforce your thoughts and learn more about what you think and believe. These are very informal movements, not like a member-

ship organizations, just a mood that involves inter-
actions among people. It has a very noticeable
effect. That's the danger of democracy: If organizations can develop, if people are no longer just glued
to the tube, you may have all these funny thoughts
arising in their heads, like sickly inhibitions
against the use of military force. That has to be
overcome, but it hasn't been overcome.

PARADE OF ENEMIES

Instead of talking about the last war, let me talk about the next war, because sometimes it's useful to be prepared instead of just reacting. There is a very characteristic development going on in the United States now. It's not the first country in the world that's done this. There are growing domestic social and economic problems, in fact, maybe catastrophes. Nobody in power has any intention of doing anything about them. If you look at the domestic programs of the administrations of the past ten years—I include here the Democratic opposition—there's really no serious proposal about what to do about the severe problems of health, education, homelessness, joblessness, crime, soaring criminal

42

populations, jails, deterioration in the inner cities—the whole raft of problems. You all know about them, and they're all getting worse. Just in the two years that George Bush has been in office three million more children crossed the poverty line, the debt is zooming, educational standards are declining, real wages are now back to the level of about the late 1950s for much of the population, and nobody's doing anything about it. In such circumstances you've got to divert the bewildered herd, because if they start noticing this they may not like it, since they're the ones suffering from it. Just having them watch the Superbowl and the sitcoms may not be enough. You have to whip them up into fear of enemies. In the 1930s Hitler whipped them into fear of the Jews and gypsies. You had to crush them to defend yourselves. We have our ways, too. Over the last ten years, every year or two, some major monster is constructed that we have to defend ourselves against. There used to be one that was always readily available: The Russians. You could always defend yourself against the Russians. But they're losing their attractiveness as an enemy, and it's getting harder and harder to use that one, so some new ones have to be conjured up. In fact, people have quite unfairly criticized George Bush for being unable to express or articulate what's really driving us now. That's very unfair. Prior to about the mid-1980s, when you were asleep you would just play the record: the Russians are coming. But he lost that one and he's got to make up new ones, just like the Reaganite public relations apparatus did in the 1980s. So it was international terrorists and narcotraffickers and crazed Arabs and Saddam Hussein, the new Hitler, was going to conquer the world. They've got to keep coming up one after another. You frighten the population, terrorize them, intimidate them so that they're too afraid to travel and cower in fear. Then you have a magnificent victory over Grenada, Panama, or some other defenseless third-world army that you can pulverize before you ever bother to look at them—which is just what happened. That gives relief. We were saved at the last minute. That's one of the ways in which you can keep the bewildered herd from paying attention to what's really going on around them, keep them diverted and controlled. The next one that's coming along, most likely, will be Cuba. That's going to require a continuation of the illegal economic warfare, possibly a revival of the extraordinary inter-

44   **NOAM CHOMSKY**

national terrorism. The most major international terrorism organized yet has been the Kennedy administration's Operation Mongoose, then the things that followed along, against Cuba. There's been nothing remotely comparable to it except perhaps the war against Nicaragua, if you call that terrorism. The World Court classified it as something more like aggression. There's always an ideological offensive that builds up a chimerical monster, then campaigns to have it crushed. You can't go in if they can fight back. That's much too dangerous. But if you are sure that they will be crushed, maybe we'll knock that one off and heave another sigh of relief.

SELECTIVE PERCEPTION

This has been going on for quite a while. In May 1986, the memoirs of the released Cuban prisoner, Armando Valladares, came out. They quickly became a media sensation. I'll give you a couple of quotes. The media described his revelations as "the definitive account of the vast system of torture and prison by which Castro punishes and obliterates political opposition." It was "an inspiring and unforgettable account" of the "bestial prisons," inhuman torture, [and] record of state violence [under] yet another of this century's mass murderers, who we learn, at last, from this book "has created a new despotism that has institutionalized torture as a mechanism of social control" in "the hell that was

46

the Cuba that [Valladares] lived in." That's the *Washington Post* and *New York Times* in repeated reviews. Castro was described as "a dictatorial goon." His atrocities were revealed in this book so conclusively that "only the most light-headed and cold-blooded Western intellectual will come to the tyrant's defense," said the *Washington Post*. Remember, this is the account of what happened to one man. Let's say it's all true. Let's raise no questions about what happened to the one man who says he was tortured. At a White House ceremony marking Human Rights Day, he was singled out by Ronald Reagan for his courage in enduring the horrors and sadism of this bloody Cuban tyrant. He was then appointed the U.S. representative at the U.N. Human Rights Commission, where he has been able to perform signal services defending the Salvadoran and Guatemalan governments against charges that they conduct atrocities so massive that they make anything he suffered look pretty minor. That's the way things stand.

That was May 1986. It was interesting, and it tells you something about the manufacture of consent. The same month, the surviving members of the Human Rights Group of El Salvador—the leaders had been killed—were arrested and tortured, including Herbert Anaya, who was the director. They were sent to a prison—La Esperanza (hope) Prison. While they were in prison they continued their human rights work. They were lawyers, they continued taking affidavits. There were 432 prisoners in that prison. They got signed affidavits from 430 of them in which they described, under oath, the torture that they had received: electrical torture and other atrocities, including, in one case, torture by a North American U.S. major in uniform, who is described in some detail. This is an unusually explicit and comprehensive testimony, probably unique in its detail about what's going on in a torture chamber. This 160–page report of the prisoners' sworn testimony was sneaked out of prison, along with a videotape which was taken showing people testifying in prison about their torture. It was distributed by the Marin County Interfaith Task Force. *The national press refused to cover it. The TV stations refused to run it.* There was an article in the local Marin County newspaper, the *San Francisco Examiner,* and I think that's all. No one else would touch it. This was a time when there was more than a few "light-headed and cold-blooded Western intellectuals"

NOAM CHOMSKY

who were singing the praises of José Napoleón Duarte and of Ronald Reagan. Anaya was not the subject of any tributes. He didn't get on Human Rights Day. He wasn't appointed to anything. He was released in a prisoner exchange and then assassinated, apparently by the U.S.-backed security forces. Very little information about that ever appeared. The media never asked whether exposure of the atrocities—instead of sitting on them and silencing them—might have saved his life.

This tells you something about the way a well-functioning system of consent manufacturing works. In comparison with the revelations of Herbert Anaya in El Salvador, Valladares's memoirs are not even a pea next to the mountain. But you've got your job to do. That takes us toward the next war. I expect, we're going to hear more and more of this, until the next operation takes place.

A few remarks about the last one. Let's turn finally to that. Let me begin with this University of Massachusetts study that I mentioned before. It has some interesting conclusions. In the study people were asked whether they thought that the United States should intervene with force to reverse illegal occupation or serious human rights abuses. By about two to one, people in the United States thought we should. We should use force in the case of illegal occupation of land and *severe* human rights abuses. If the United States was to follow that advice, we would bomb El Salvador, Guatemala, Indonesia, Damascus, Tel Aviv, Capetown, Turkey, Washington, and a whole list of other states. These are all cases of illegal occupation and aggression and severe human rights abuses. If you know the facts about that range of examples, you'll know very well that Saddam Hussein's aggression and atrocities fall well within the range. They're not the most extreme. Why doesn't anybody come to that conclusion? The reason is that nobody knows. In a well-functioning propaganda system, nobody would know what I'm talking about when I list that range of examples. If you bother to look, you find that those examples are quite appropriate.

Take one that was ominously close to being perceived during the Gulf War. In February, right in the middle of the bombing campaign, the government of Lebanon requested Israel to observe U.N. Security Council Resolution 425, which called on it to withdraw immediately and unconditionally from Lebanon. That resolution dates from March

1978. There have since been two subsequent resolutions calling for the immediate and unconditional withdrawal of Israel from Lebanon. Of course it doesn't observe them because the United States backs it in maintaining that occupation. Meanwhile southern Lebanon is terrorized. There are big torture-chambers with horrifying things going on. It's used as a base for attacking other parts of Lebanon. Since 1978, Lebanon was invaded, the city of Beirut was bombed, about 20,000 people were killed, about 80 percent of them civilians, hospitals were destroyed, and more terror, looting, and robbery was inflicted. All fine, the United States backed it. That's just one case. You didn't see anything in the media about it or any discussion about whether Israel and the United States should observe U.N. Security Council Resolution 425 or any of the other resolutions, nor did anyone call for the bombing of Tel Aviv, although by the principles upheld by two-thirds of the population, we should. After all, that's illegal occupation and severe human rights abuses. That's just one case. There are much worse ones. The Indonesian invasion of East Timor knocked off about 200,000 people. They all look minor by that one. That was strongly backed by the United States and is *still* going on with major United States diplomatic and military support. We can go on and on.

THE GULF WAR

That tells you how a well-functioning propaganda system works. People can believe that when we use force against Iraq and Kuwait it's because we really observe the principle that illegal occupation and human rights abuses should be met by force. They don't see what it would mean if those principles were applied to U.S. behavior. That's a success of propaganda of quite a spectacular type.

Let's take a look at another case. If you look closely at the coverage of the war since August (1990), you'll notice that there are a couple of striking voices missing. For example, there is an Iraqi democratic opposition, in fact, a very courageous and quite substantial Iraqi democratic opposition.

They, of course, function in exile because they couldn't survive in Iraq. They are in Europe primarily. They are bankers, engineers, architects—people like that. They are articulate, they have voices, and they speak. The previous February, when Saddam Hussein was still George Bush's favorite friend and trading partner, they actually came to Washington, according to Iraqi democratic opposition sources, with a plea for some kind of support for a demand of theirs calling for a parliamentary democracy in Iraq. They were totally rebuffed, because the United States had no interest in it. There was no reaction to this in the public record.

Since August it became a little harder to ignore their existence. In August we suddenly turned against Saddam Hussein after having favored him for many years. Here was an Iraqi democratic opposition who ought to have some thoughts about the matter. They would be happy to see Saddam Hussein drawn and quartered. He killed their brothers, tortured their sisters, and drove them out of the country. They have been fighting against his tyranny throughout the whole time that Ronald Reagan and George Bush were cherishing him. What about their voices? Take a look at the national media and see how much you can find about the Iraqi democratic opposition from August through March (1991). You can't find a word. It's not that they're inarticulate. They have statements, proposals, calls and demands. If you look at them, you find that they're indistinguishable from those of the American peace movement. They're against Saddam Hussein and they're against the war against Iraq. They don't want their country destroyed. What they want is a peaceful resolution, and they knew perfectly well that it might have been achievable. That's the wrong view and therefore they're out. We don't hear a word about the Iraqi democratic opposition. If you want to find out about them, pick up the German press, or the British press. They don't say much about them, but they're less controlled than we are and they say something.

This is a spectacular achievement of propaganda. First, that the voices of the Iraqi democrats are completely excluded, and second, that nobody notices it. That's interesting, too. It takes a really deeply indoctrinated population not to notice that we're not hearing the voices of the Iraqi democratic opposition and not asking the question, Why? and finding out the obvious answer: because the Iraqi democrats have their own thoughts; they agree with the international peace movement and therefore they're out.

Let's take the question of the reasons for the war. Reasons were offered for the war. The reasons are: aggressors cannot be rewarded and aggression must be reversed by the quick resort to violence; that was the reason for the war. There was basically no other reason advanced. Can that possibly be the reason for the war? Does the United States uphold those principles, that aggressors cannot be rewarded and that aggression must be reversed by a quick resort to violence? I won't insult your intelligence by running through the facts, but the fact is those arguments could be refuted in two minutes by a literate teenager. However, they never were refuted. Take a look at the media, the liberal commentators and critics, the people who testified in Congress and see whether anybody questioned the assumption that the United States stands up to those principles. Has the United States opposed its own aggression in Panama and insisted on bombing Washington to reverse it? When the South African occupation of Namibia was declared illegal in 1969, did the United States impose sanctions on food and medicine? Did it go to war? Did it bomb Capetown? No, it carried out twenty years of "quiet diplomacy." It wasn't very pretty during those twenty years. In the years of the Reagan-Bush administration alone, about 1.5 million people were killed by South Africa just in the surrounding countries. Forget what was happening in South Africa and Namibia. Somehow that didn't sear our sensitive souls. We continued with "quite diplomacy" and ended up with ample reward for the aggressors. They were given the major port in Namibia and plenty of advantages that took into account their security concerns. Where is this principle that we uphold? Again, it's child's play to demonstrate that those couldn't possibly have been the reasons for going to war, because we don't uphold these principles. But nobody did it—that's what's important. And nobody bothered to point out the conclusion that follows: No reason was given for going to war. None. No reason was given for going to war that could not be refuted by a literate teenager in about two minutes. That again is the hallmark of a totalitarian culture. It ought to frighten us, that we are so deeply totalitarian that we can be driven to war without any reason being given for it and without anybody noticing Lebanon's request or caring. It's a very striking fact.

Right before the bombing started, in mid-January, a major *Washington Post*-ABC poll revealed something interesting. People were asked, If Iraq would agree to withdraw from Kuwait in return for Security Council consideration of the problem of Arab-Israeli conflict, would you be in favor of that? By about two-to-one, the population was in favor of that. So was the whole world, including the Iraqi democratic opposition. So it was reported that two-thirds of the American population were in favor of that. Presumably, the people who were in favor of that thought they were the only ones in the world to think so. Certainly nobody in the press had said that it would be a good idea. The orders from Washington have been, we're supposed to be against "linkage," that is, diplomacy, and therefore everybody goose-stepped on command and everybody was against diplomacy. Try to find commentary in the press—you can find a column by Alex Cockburn in the *Los Angeles Times*, who argued that it would be a good idea. The people who were answering that question thought, I'm alone, but that's what I think. Suppose they knew that they weren't alone, that other people thought it, like the Iraqi democratic opposition. Suppose that they knew that this was not hypothetical, that in fact Iraq had made exactly such an offer. It had been released by high U.S. officials just eight days earlier. On January 2, these officials had released an Iraqi offer to withdraw totally from Kuwait in return for consideration by the Security Council of the Arab-Israeli conflict and the problem of weapons of mass destruction. The United States had been refusing to negotiate this issue since well before the invasion of Kuwait. Suppose that people had known that the offer was actually on the table and that it was widely supported and that in fact it's exactly the kind of thing that any rational person would do if they were interested in peace, as we do in other cases, in the rare cases that we do want to reverse aggression. Suppose that it had been known. You can make your own guesses, but I would assume that the two-thirds would probably have risen to 98 percent of the population. Here you have the great successes of propaganda. Probably not one person who answered the poll knew any of the things I've just mentioned. The people thought they were alone. Therefore it was possible to proceed with the war policy without opposition.

There was a good deal of discussion about whether sanctions would work. You had the head of the CIA come up and discuss whether sanctions would work. However, there was no discussion of a much more obvious question: Had sanctions already worked? The answer is yes, apparently they had— probably by late August, very likely by late December. It was very hard to think up any other reason for the Iraqi offers of withdrawal, which were authenticated or in some cases released by high U.S. officials, who described them as "serious" and "negotiable." So the real question is: Had sanctions already worked? Was there a way out? Was there a way out in terms quite acceptable to the general population, the world at large and the Iraqi democratic opposition? These questions were not discussed, and it's crucial for a well-functioning propaganda system that they *not* be discussed. That enables the chairman of the Republican National Committee to say that if any Democrat had been in office, Kuwait would not be liberated today. He can say that and no Democrat would get up and say that if I were president it would have been liberated not only today but six months ago, because there were opportunities then that I would have pursued and Kuwait would have been liberated without killing tens of thousands of people and without causing an environmental catastrophe. No Democrat would say that because no Democrat took that position. Henry Gonzalez and Barbara Boxer took that position. But the number of people who took it is so marginal that it's virtually nonexistent. Given the fact that almost no Democratic politician would say that, Clayton Yeutter is free to make his statements.

When Scud missiles hit Israel, nobody in the press applauded. Again, that's an interesting fact about a well-functioning propaganda system. We might ask, why not? After all, Saddam Hussein's arguments were as good as George Bush's arguments. What were they, after all? Let's just take Lebanon. Saddam Hussein says that he can't stand annexation. He can't let Israel annex the Syrian Golan Heights and East Jerusalem, in opposition to the unanimous agreement of the Security Council. He can't stand annexation. He can't stand aggression. Israel has been occupying southern Lebanon since 1978 in violation of Security Council resolutions that it refuses to abide by. In the course of that period it attacked all of Lebanon, still bombs most of Lebanon at will. He can't stand it. He might have read the Amnesty International report on Israeli atrocities in the West Bank. His heart is bleeding. He can't stand it. Sanctions can't work because the United States vetoes them. Negotiations won't work because the United States blocks them. What's left but force? He's been waiting for years. Thirteen years in the case of Lebanon, 20 years in the case of the West Bank. You've heard that argument before. The only difference between that argument and the one you heard is that Saddam Hussein could truly say sanctions and negotiations can't work because the United States blocks them. But George Bush couldn't say that, because sanctions apparently had worked, and there was every reason to believe that negotiations could work—except that he adamantly refused to pursue them, saying explicitly, there will be no negotiations right through. Did you find anybody in the press who pointed that out? No. It's a triviality. It's something that, again, a literate teenager could figure out in a minute. But nobody pointed it out, no commentator, no editorial writer. That, again, is the sign of a very well-run totalitarian culture. It shows that the manufacture of consent is working.

Last comment about this. We could give many examples, you could make them up as you go along. Take the idea that Saddam Hussein is a monster about to conquer the world—widely believed, in the United States, and not unrealistically. It was drilled into people's heads over and over again: He's about to take everything. We've got to stop him now. How did he get that powerful? This is a small, third-world country without an industrial base. For eight years Iraq had been fighting Iran. That's post-revolutionary Iran, which had decimated its officer corps and most of its military force. Iraq had a little bit of support in that war. It was backed by the Soviet Union, the United States, Europe, the major Arab countries, and the Arab oil producers. It couldn't defeat Iran. But all of a sudden it's ready to conquer the world. Did you find anybody who pointed that out? The fact of the matter is, this was a third-world country with a peasant army. It is now being conceded that there was a ton of disinformation about the fortifications, the chemical weapons, etc. But did you find anybody who pointed it out? No. You found virtually nobody who pointed it out. That's typical. Notice that this was done one year after exactly the same thing was done with Manuel Noriega. Manuel Noriega is a minor thug by comparison with George Bush's friend Saddam Hussein or George Bush's other friends in Beijing or George Bush himself, for that matter. In comparison with them, Manuel Noriega is a pretty minor thug. Bad, but not a world-class thug of the kind we like. He was turned into a creature larger than life. He was going to destroy us, leading the narco-traffickers. We had to quickly move in and smash him, killing a couple hundred or maybe thousand people, restoring to power the tiny, maybe eight percent white oligarchy, and putting U.S. military officers in control at every level of the political system. We had to do all those things because, after all, we had to save ourselves or we were going to be destroyed by this monster. One year later the same thing was done by Saddam Hussein. Did anybody point it out? Did anybody point out what had happened or why? You'll have to look pretty hard for that.

Notice that this is not all that different from what the Creel Commission when it turned a pacifistic population into raving hysterics who wanted to destroy everything German to save ourselves from Huns who were tearing the arms off Belgian babies. The techniques are maybe more sophisticated, with television and lots of money going into it, but it's pretty traditional.

I think the issue, to come back to my original comment, is not simply disinformation and the Gulf crisis. The issue is much broader. It's whether we want to live in a free society or whether we want to live under what amounts to a form of self-imposed totalitarianism, with the bewildered herd marginalized, directed elsewhere, terrified, screaming patriotic slogans, fearing for their lives and admiring with awe the leader who saved them from destruction, while the educated masses goose-step on command and repeat the slogans they're supposed to repeat and the society deteriorates at home. We end up serving as a mercenary enforcer state, hoping that others are going to pay us to smash up the world. Those are the choices. That's the choice that you have to face. The answer to those questions is very much in the hands of people like *you* and *me*.

Notes

1. *New York Times*, 18 October1985.
2. *Washington Post*, 26 October 1984.
3. See essays by Jack Spence and Eldon Kenworthy in Thomas Walker, ed., *Reagan vs. the Sandinistas* (Boulder: Westview, 1987).
4. See Noam Chomsky, *Necessary Illusions* (Boston: South End, 1989), for some comment and sources.

5. *Liberation*, September-October 1967. Reprinted in Noam Chomsky, *American Power and the New Mandarins* (New York: Pantheon, 1969).
6. *Envío*, March 1994.
7. *Jerusalem Post*, 16 August 1981.
8. *Washington Post Weekly*, 14 March 1988.

THE JOURNALIST FROM MARS

How the "War on Terror" Should Be Reported

The following text is an edited transcript of a talk given at Fairness
and Accuracy in Reporting's fifteenth anniversary celebration at
Town Hall, New York City, January 22, 2002.

THE PROPER TOPIC FOR an occasion like this, I suppose, is pretty obvious: It would be the question of how the media have handled the major story of the past months, the issue of the "war on terrorism," so-called, specifically in the Islamic world. Incidentally, by media here I intend the term to be understood pretty broadly, including journals of commentary, analysis, and opinion; in fact, the intellectual culture generally.

It's a really important topic. It's been reviewed regularly by FAIR, among others. However, it isn't really an appropriate topic for a talk, and the reason is that it requires too much detailed analysis. So what I'd like to do is take a somewhat different approach to it and ask the question of how should the story be handled, in accord with general principles that are accepted as guidelines: principles of fairness, accuracy, relevance, and so on.

Let's approach this by kind of a thought experiment. Imagine an intelligent Martian—I'm told that by convention, Martians are males, so I'll refer to it as "he." Suppose that this Martian went to Harvard and Columbia Journalism School and learned all kinds of high-minded things, and actually believes them. How would the Martian handle a story like this?

I think he would begin with some factual observations that he'd send back to the journal on Mars. One factual observation is that the war on terrorism was not declared on September 11; rather, it was redeclared, using the same rhetoric as the first declaration twenty years earlier. The Reagan administration, as you know, I'm sure, came into office announcing that a war on terrorism would be the core of U.S. foreign policy, and it condemned what the president called the "evil scourge of terrorism."[1] The main focus was state-supported international terrorism in the Islamic world, and at that time also in Central America. International terrorism was described as a plague spread by "depraved opponents of civilization itself," in "a return to barbarism in the modern age."[2] Actually, I'm quoting the administration moderate, Secretary of State George Shultz.

The phrase I quoted from Reagan had to do with terrorism in the Middle East, and it was the year 1985. That was the year in which international terrorism in that region was selected by editors as the lead story of the year in an annual Associated Press poll, so point one that our Martian would report is that the year 2001 is the second time that this has been the main lead story, and that the war on terrorism has been redeclared pretty much as before.

Furthermore, there's a striking continuity; the same people are in leading positions. So Donald Rumsfeld is running the military component of the second phase of the war on terrorism, and he was Reagan's special envoy to the Middle East during the first phase of the war on terrorism, including the peak year, 1985. The person who was just appointed a couple of months ago to be in charge of the diplomatic component of the war at the United Nations is John Negroponte, who during the first phase was supervising U.S. operations in Honduras, which was the main base for the U.S. war against terror in the first phase.

Exercising the Power Element

In 1985, terrorism in the Middle East was the lead story, but terrorism in Central America had second rank as the story of the day. Shultz, in fact, regarded the plague in Central America as what he called the most alarming manifestation of it. The main problem, he explained, was "a cancer right here in our hemisphere,"[3] and we want to cut it out and we'd better do it fast because the cancer was openly proclaiming the goals of Hitler's *Mein Kampf* and was just about to take over the world. And it was really dangerous. The danger was so severe that on Law Day 1985, the president announced a state of national emergency because of, as he put it, "the unusual and extraordinary threat to the national security and foreign policy of the United States" posed by this cancer. (Law Day, incidentally, is the day that in the rest of the world is commemorated as a day in solidarity with the struggles of American workers. In the United States it's a jingoist holiday, May 1.)

This state of emergency was renewed annually until finally the cancer was cut out. Secretary of

State Shultz explained that the danger was so severe that you can't keep to gentle means; in his words (April 14, 1986), "Negotiations are a euphemism for capitulation if the shadow of power is not cast across the bargaining table." He condemned those who "seek utopian legalistic means like outside mediation, the United Nations, and the World Court while ignoring the power element of the equation."

The United States had been, in fact, exercising the power element of the equation with mercenary forces based in Honduras, under the supervision of John Negroponte, while it was successfully blocking pursuit of utopian legalistic means by the World Court, the Latin American countries, and of course the cancer itself, bent on world conquest.

The media agreed. The only question that arose, really, was tactics. There was the usual hawk/dove debate. The position of the hawks was expressed pretty well by the editors of *The New Republic* (April 4, 1984). They demanded, in their words, that we continue to send military aid to "Latin-style fascists...regardless of how many are murdered," because "there are higher American priorities than Salvadoran human rights," or anywhere else in the region. That's the hawks.

The doves argued, on the other hand, that these means were just not going to work, and they proposed alternative means to return Nicaragua, the cancer, to the "Central American mode" and impose "regional standards" on it. I'm quoting the *Washington Post* (March 14, 1986; March 19, 1986). The Central American mode and the regional standards were those of the terror states El Salvador and Guatemala, which were at that time massacring, torturing, and devastating in ways I don't have to describe. So we had to return Nicaragua to the Central American mode as well, according to the doves.

The op-eds and editorials in the national press were divided on this roughly fifty-fifty between the hawks and the doves. There were exceptions, but they're literally at the level of statistical error. There's material on this in print, and there has been for a long time if you want to take a look.[4] In the other major region where the plague was raging at that time, in the Middle East, uniformity was even more extreme.

Same War, Different targets

Well, the intelligent Martian would certainly pay great attention to all of this very recent history, in fact with remarkable continuity, so that the front pages on Mars would report that the so-called war on terror is redeclared by the same people against rather similar targets, although, he would point out, not quite the same targets.

The depraved opponents of civilization itself in the year 2001 were in the 1980s the freedom fighters organized and armed by the CIA and its associates, trained by the same special forces who are now searching for them in caves in Afghanistan. They were a component of the first war against terror and acting pretty much the same way as the other components of the war against terror.

They didn't hide their terrorist agenda that began early on, in fact in 1981, when they assassinated the President of Egypt, and is continuing. That included terrorist attacks inside Russia severe enough so that at one point they virtually led to a war with Pakistan, although these attacks stopped after the Russians withdrew from Afghanistan in 1989, leaving the ravaged country in the hands of the U.S. favorites, who turned at once to mass murder, rape, terror—generally described as the worst period in Afghanistan's history. They're now back in charge outside of Kabul. According to this morning's *Wall*

Street Journal (January 22, 2001), two of the major warlords are now approaching what could turn out to be a major war. Let's hope not.

All of this is headline news in the Martian press—along, of course, with what it all means to the civilian population. That includes vast numbers of people who are still deprived of desperately needed food and other supplies, although food has been available for months but can't be distributed because of conditions; that's after four months.

The consequences of that we don't know, and in fact will never know. Because there's a principle of the intellectual culture that although you investigate enemy crimes with laserlike intensity, you never look at your own—that's quite important—so we can only give very vague estimates of the number of Vietnamese or Salvadoran or other corpses that we've left around.

The Heresy of Moral Equivalence

As I say, this would be headlines on Mars. A good Martian reporter would also want to clarify a couple of basic ideas. First of all, he'd like to know what exactly is terrorism. And, secondly, what's the proper response to it. Well, whatever the answer to the second question is, that proper response must satisfy some moral truisms, and the Martian can easily discover what these truisms are, at least as understood by the leaders of the self-declared war on terrorism, because they tell us, they tell us constantly, that they are very pious Christians, who therefore revere the Gospels, and have certainly memorized the definition of "hypocrite" given prominently in the Gospels—namely, the hypocrites are those who apply to others the standards that they refuse to accept for themselves.

So the Martian understands, then, that in order to rise to the absolutely minimal moral level we have to agree, in fact insist, that if some act is right for us then it's right for others, and if it's wrong when others do it then it's wrong when we do it. Now that's the most elementary of moral truisms, and once the Martian realizes that, he can pack up his bags and go back to Mars. Because his research task is over. He would be unlikely to find a phrase, a single phrase in the vast coverage and commentary about the war on terrorism that even begins to approach this minimal standard. Don't take my word for it; try the experiment. I don't want to exaggerate—you can probably find the phrase now and then, way out at the margins, though very rarely.

Nevertheless, this moral truism is recognized within the mainstream. It's understood to be an extremely dangerous heresy, and therefore it's necessary to erect impregnable barriers against it, even before anybody exhibits it, even though it's so rare. In fact, there's even a technical vocabulary available in case anybody would dare to engage in the heresy, to involve themselves in the heresy that we should abide by moral truisms that we pretend to revere. The offenders are guilty of something called moral relativism—that means the suggestion that we apply to ourselves the standards we apply to others. Or maybe moral equivalence, which is a term that was invented, I think, by Jeane Kirkpatrick to ward off the danger that somebody might dare to look at our own crimes.

Or maybe they're carrying out the crime of America-bashing, or they're anti-Americans. Which is a rather interesting concept. The term is used elsewhere only in totalitarian states, for example in Russia in the old days, where anti-Sovietism was the highest crime. If somebody were to publish a book in Italy, say, called *The Anti-Italians*, you can imagine what the reaction would be in the streets of Milan and Rome, or in any country where freedom and democracy were taken seriously.

An Unusable Definition

But let's suppose that the Martian isn't deterred by the inevitable tirades and stream of vilification, and suppose he persists in keeping to the most elementary moral truisms. Well, as I said, if he does that, he can just go home, but suppose out of curiosity he decides to stay on and look a little bit further. So, what will happen? Well, back to the question, what is terrorism?—an important one.

There is a proper course for a serious Martian reporter to follow to find the answer to that: Look at the people who declared the war on terrorism and see what they say terrorism is; that's fair enough. And there is in fact an official definition in the U.S. code and Army manuals, and elsewhere. It is defined briefly. Terrorism, as I'm quoting, is defined as "the calculated use of violence or the threat of violence to attain goals that are political, religious or ideological in nature...through intimidation, coercion or instilling fear." Well, that sounds simple; as far as I can see, it's appropriate. But we constantly read that the problem of defining terrorism is very vexing and complex, and the Martian might wonder why that's true. And there's an answer.

The official definition is unusable. It's unusable for two important reasons. First of all, it's a very close paraphrase of official government policy—very close, in fact. When it's government policy, it's called low-intensity conflict or counterterror.

Incidentally, it's not just the United States. As far as I'm aware, this practice is universal. Just as an example, back in the mid 1960s the Rand Corporation, the research agency connected with the Pentagon mostly, published a collection of interesting Japanese counterinsurgency manuals having to do with the Japanese attack on Manchuria and North China in the 1930s. I was kind of interested—I wrote an article on it at the time comparing the Japanese counterinsurgency manuals with U.S. counterinsurgency manuals for South Vietnam, which are virtually identical.[5] That article didn't fly too well, I should say.

Well, anyhow, it's a fact, and as far as I know it's a universal fact. So that's one reason you can't use the official definition. The other reason you can't do it is much simpler: it just gives all the wrong answers, radically so, as to who the terrorists are.

So therefore the official definition has to be abandoned, and you have to search for some kind of sophisticated definition that will give the right answers, and that's hard. That's why you hear that it's such a difficult topic and big minds are wrestling with it and so on.

Fortunately, there is a solution. The solution is to define terrorism as the terrorism that they carry out against us, whoever we happen to be. As far as I know, that's universal—in journalism, in scholarship, and also I think it's a historical universal; at least, I've never found any country that doesn't follow this practice. So, fortunately, there's a way out of the problem. Well, with this useful characterization of terrorism, we can then draw the standard conclusions that you read all the time: namely, that we and our allies are the main victims of terrorism, and that terrorism is a weapon of the weak.

Of course, terrorism in the official sense is a weapon of the strong, like most weapons, but it's a weapon of the weak, by definition, once you comprehend that "terrorism" just means the terrorism that they carry out against us. Then of course it's true by definition that terrorism is a weapon of the weak. And so the people who write it all the time, you see it in the newspapers or the journals, they're right; it's a tautology, and by convention.

Textbook Terrorism

Suppose the Martian goes on to defy what are apparently universal conventions, and he actually accepts the moral truisms that are preached and he also even accepts the official U.S. definition of terrorism. I should say that by this time he's way out in outer space, but let's proceed. If he goes this far, then there certainly are clear illustrations of terrorism. September 11, for example, is a particularly shocking example of a terrorist atrocity. Another equally clear example is the official U.S.-British reaction, which was announced by Admiral Sir Michael Boyce, chief of the British defense staff, and reported in a front- page story in the *New York Times* in late October (October 28, 2001). He informed the people of Afghanistan that the United States and Britain would continue their attack against them "until they get the leadership changed."

Notice that this is a textbook illustration of international terrorism, according to the official definition; I won't reread it but if you think about it, it's just a perfect illustration.

Two weeks before that, George Bush had informed the Afghans, the people of Afghanistan, that the attack will go on until they hand over wanted suspects. Remember that overthrow of the Taliban regime was a sort of afterthought brought in a couple of weeks after the bombing, basically for the benefit of intellectuals so they could write about how just the war is.

This of course was also textbook terrorism: We're going to continue to bomb you until you hand over some people we want you to hand over. The Taliban regime did ask for evidence, but the U.S. contemptuously dismissed that request. The U.S., at the very same time, also flatly refused to even consider offers of extradition, which may have been serious, may not have been; we don't know because they were rejected.

The Martian would certainly record all of this, and if he did a little homework he would quickly find the reasons, adding many other examples. The reasons are very simple: The world's rulers have to make it clear that they do not defer to any authority. Therefore they do not accept the idea that they should offer evidence, they do not agree that they should request extradition; in fact, they reject UN

Security Council authorization, reject it flatly. The U.S. could easily have obtained clear and unambiguous authorization—not for pretty reasons, but it could have obtained it. However, it rejected that option.

And that makes good sense. In fact, there's even a term for this in the literature of international affairs and diplomacy. It's called establishing credibility. Another term for it is declaring that we're a terrorist state and you'd better be aware of the consequences if you get in our way. Now that's, of course, only if we use "terrorism" in its official sense, as it's defined in U.S. government legal code and so on, and that's unacceptable for reasons that I mentioned.

Uncontroversial Cases

Let's go back to the moral truism. According to official doctrine, which is almost universally accepted and described as just and admirable and obviously so, the United States is entitled to conduct a terrorist war against Afghans until they hand over suspects to the United States, which refuses to provide evidence or request extradition, or, in Boyce's later terms, until they change their leadership. Well, anyone who is not a hypocrite in the sense of the Gospels will therefore conclude at once that Haiti is entitled to carry out large-scale terrorism against the United States until it hands over a murderer, Emmanuel Constant, who has already been convicted of leading the terrorist forces that had the major responsibility for four to five thousand deaths.

No question about the evidence in this case. They've requested extradition repeatedly, most recently on September 30, 2001, right in the midst of all the talk about Afghanistan being subjected to terrorism if it doesn't hand over suspected terrorists. Of course, that's only four or five thousand black people. I guess it doesn't count quite as much.

Or perhaps they should carry out massive terror in the United States. Since they can't bomb, maybe bioterror or something, I don't know, until the United States changes its leadership, which is, in fact, responsible for terrible crimes against the people of Haiti right through the twentieth century.

Or certainly, keeping now to moral truisms, Nicaragua is entitled to do the same, incidentally targeting the leaders of the redeclared war on terrorism, the same people often. Recall that the terrorist attack against Nicaragua was far more severe than even September 11; tens of thousands of people were killed, the country was devastated, it may never recover.

Also, this happens to be an uncontroversial example, so we don't have to argue about it. It's uncontroversial because of the judgment of the World Court condemning the United States for international terrorism, backed up by the Security Council in a resolution calling on all states to observe international law—mentioning no one, but everyone knew who they meant—vetoed by the United States, Britain abstaining. Or the judgment of the General Assembly in successive resolutions confirming the same thing, opposed by the United States and one or two client states. The World Court ordered the United States to terminate the crime of international terrorism, to pay massive reparations. The U.S. responded with a bipartisan decision to escalate the attack immediately; I already described the media reaction. All of this continued until the cancer was destroyed and it continues right now.

So in November 2001 there was an election in

Nicaragua, right in the middle of the war on terrorism, and the United States radically intervened in the election. It warned Nicaragua that the United States would not accept the wrong outcome, and even gave the reason. The State Department explained that we cannot overlook Nicaragua's role in international terrorism in the 1980s, when it resisted the international terrorist attack that led to the condemnation of the United States for international terrorism by the highest international authorities.

Here all of this passes without comment in an intellectual culture that is simply dedicated passionately to terrorism and hypocrisy, but I guess it might have had some headlines in the Martian press. You might look and see how it was treated here. You might also incidentally try out your favorite theory of "just war" in this uncontroversial case.

Domesticating the Majority

Nicaragua, of course, had some defense against the U.S.-run international terrorism being carried out against it under the pretext of a war on terrorism. Namely, Nicaragua had an army. In the other Central American countries, the terrorist forces that were armed and trained by the U.S. and its clients were the army, so not surprisingly the terrorist atrocities were far worse. That's the Central American mode that the doves said we have to return the cancer to. But in this case the victims weren't the state, and therefore they could not appeal to the World Court or to the Security Council for judgments that would be rejected, tossed into the ashcan of history, except maybe on Mars.

The effects of that terror were long-lasting. Here in the United States, there's a good deal of concern—very properly as a matter of fact—about the very wide-ranging effects of the terrorist atrocities of September 11. So, for example, there's a front-page article in the *New York Times* (January 22, 2002) about the people who are beyond the reach of benefits for the tragedy that they suffered. Of course, the same is true for those who are victims of vastly worse terrorist crimes, but that's reported only on Mars.

So you might try to find the report, say, of a conference run by Salvadoran Jesuits a couple of years ago. The Jesuits' experiences under U.S. international terrorism were particularly grisly. The conference report[6] stressed the residual effect of what it called the culture of terrorism, which domesticates the aspirations of the majority, who realized that they must submit to the dictates of the ruling terrorist state and its local agents or they will again be returned to the Central American mode, as recommended by the doves at the peak of the state-supported international terrorism of the eighties. Unreported here, of course; maybe headlines on Mars.

Enthusiastic Partners

Actually, the Martian might notice some other interesting similarities between the first and the second phase of the war on terror. In the year 2001, just about every terrorist state you think of was eagerly joining in the coalition against terrorism, and the reasons are not hidden.

We all know why the Russians are so enthusiastic: they want U.S. endorsement for their monstrous terrorist activities in Chechnya, for example.

Turkey was particularly enthusiastic. They were the first country to offer troops, and the prime minister explained why. This was in gratitude for the fact that the United States alone was willing to pour arms into Turkey—providing eighty percent of their arms in the Clinton years—in order to enable them to expedite some of the worst terrorist atrocities and ethnic cleansing of the 1990s. And they're very grateful for that, and so they offered troops for the new war on terrorism. Incidentally, none of this counts as terrorism, remember, because by the convention, since we're carrying it out it's not terrorism. And so on down the list; I won't go through the rest.

And the same, incidentally, was true of the first phase of the war on terrorism. So the announcement by Admiral Boyce that I quoted was a close paraphrase of words of the well-known Israeli statesman Abba Eban in 1981. That was shortly after the first war against terrorism was declared. Eban was justifying Israeli atrocities in Lebanon, which he acknowledged were pretty awful, but justified, he said, because "there was a rational prospect that affected populations would exert pressure for a cessation of hostilities."[7] Notice that's another textbook illustration of international terrorism in the official sense.

The hostilities that he was talking about were at the Israel-Lebanon border, overwhelmingly Israeli in origin, often without even a pretext, but backed by the United States, so therefore they're not terrorism by convention and they're not part of the history of terrorism. At the time, with decisive U.S. support,

Israel was carrying out attacks in Lebanon, bombing and other atrocities, to try to elicit some pretext for a planned invasion. Well, they couldn't get the pretext, but they invaded anyway, killing about eighteen thousand people and continuing to occupy southern Lebanon for about twenty years with many atrocities, but all off the record because the U.S. was decisively supporting it.

Prize Atrocities

All of this peaked—the post-1982 attack, in 1985, and that was the peak year for U.S.-Israeli atrocities in southern Lebanon, what were called the Iron Fist operations; these were large-scale massacres and deportations of what the high command called "terrorist villagers." These operations, under Prime Minister Shimon Peres, are one of the candidates for the prize of the worst international terrorist crime in the peak year of 1985, remember, when terrorism was the leading story of the year.

There are other competitors. One of them, also in early 1985, was a bombing in Beirut, a car bombing. The car bombing was outside a mosque timed to go off just when everybody was leaving to insure the maximum number of casualties. It killed eighty people and wounded more than two hundred fifty, according to the *Washington Post*,[8] which gave a pretty grisly account of it. Most of them were women and girls, but it was a heavy, strong bomb, so it killed infants in their beds and all kinds of other atrocities. But that doesn't count, because it was organized by the CIA and British intelligence, so therefore it's not terrorism. So that's not really a candidate for the prize.

Now, the only possible other competitor in the peak year of 1985 was the Israeli bombing of Tunis, which killed seventy-five people; there were some grisly accounts of it in the Israeli press by good reporters. The U.S. cooperated in the atrocity by failing to inform its Tunisian ally that the bombers were on their way. George Shultz, secretary of state, immediately called the Israeli prime minister, Yitzhak Shamir, to inform him that the United States had considerable sympathy for this action, as he put it. However, Shultz drew back from open support for this international terrorism when the Security Council condemned it unanimously as an act of armed aggression, with the U.S. abstaining.

Let's continue to give Washington and its clients the benefit of the doubt, as in the case of Nicaragua, and let's assume that the crime was only international terrorism, not the far more serious crime of aggression, as the Security Council determined. If it was aggression, then, observing moral truisms, we move on to Nuremburg trials.

Those are the only three cases that come anywhere near that level in the peak year of 1985. A couple of weeks after the Tunis bombing, Prime Minister Peres came to Washington, where he joined Ronald Reagan in denouncing "the evil scourge of terrorism" in the Middle East. None of this elicited a word of comment, and that's correct because by convention none of it is terrorism. Recall the convention: It's only terrorism if they do it to us. When we do much worse to them, it's not terrorism. Again, the universal principle. Well, the Martian might notice that, even if it's not discussable here.

I got my favorite review in history when I did write about this some years ago. It was a review in the *Washington Post* (September 18, 1988), a two-word review by their Middle East correspondent, who described it as "breathlessly deranged." I kind of like that. I think he was wrong about the breathless—if you read the article, it was pretty calm—but deranged is correct. I mean, you have to be deranged to accept elementary moral truisms and to describe facts that shouldn't be described. That's probably true.

Contemptible Excuses

Let's get back to the Martian. He might be puzzled about the question of why 1985 is the peak year for the return to barbarism in our time by depraved opponents of civilization itself, referring to international terrorism in the Middle East. He'd be puzzled because the worst cases by far of international terrorism in the region just are down the memory hole, like international terrorism in Central America. And lots of other cases. Current ones, in fact.

However, some cases from 1985 are remembered, well remembered, and rightly, because they are terrorism. The official prize for terrorism for that year goes to the hijacking of the *Achille Lauro* and the murder of a crippled American, Leon Klinghoffer. Everyone knows about that one. Correctly; it was a terrible atrocity. Now, of course, the perpetrators of that atrocity described it as retaliation for the Tunis bombing a week earlier, a vastly worse case of international terrorism, but quite rightly we dismissed that excuse with the contempt that it deserves.

And all of those who do not regard themselves as cowards and hypocrites will take the same principled stand with regard to all other violent acts of retaliation, including, for example, the war in Afghanistan, which remember was undertaken with the clear and unambiguous expectation that it might drive millions of people over the edge of starvation. As I said, we'll never know. For principled reasons.

Or lesser atrocities, such as those retaliations in the Israeli-occupied territories right now—with full U.S. support, as always, so they're not terrorism. The Martian would surely report on page one that the United States right now is once again using the pretext of the war on terror to protect and probably escalate terrorism by its leading client state.

The latest phase of this began on October 1, 2000. From October 1, the first days after the current Intifada began, Israeli helicopters began to attack unarmed Palestinians with missiles, killing and wounding dozens of them. There wasn't any pretext of self-defense. [Side comment: When you read the phrase "Israeli helicopters" you should understand it to mean U.S. helicopters with Israeli pilots, provided in the certain knowledge of how they are going to be used.]

Clinton immediately responded to the atrocity. On October 3, 2000, two days later, he arranged to send Israel the largest shipment of military helicopters in a decade along with spare parts for Apache attack helicopters that had been sent in mid-September. The press cooperated by refusing to report any of this—not failing, notice, but refusing; they knew all about it.

Last month the Martian press would certainly have headlined Washington's intervention to expedite the further escalation of the cycle of terror there. On December 14, the U.S. vetoed a Security Council resolution calling for implementation of the Mitchell proposals and sending international observers to monitor reduction of violence. It went at once to the General Assembly, where it was opposed by the U.S. and Israel also; therefore, it disappears. And you can check the coverage.

A week earlier, there was a conference in Geneva of the high contracting parties of the Fourth Geneva Convention, who are obliged by solemn treaty to enforce it. The Convention, as you know, was instituted after World War II to criminalize the atrocities of the Nazis. The Convention strictly bars virtually everything the U.S. and Israel do in the occupied territories, including the settlements that were established and expanded with U.S. funding and full support, increasing under Clinton and Barak during the Camp David negotiations. Israel alone rejects this interpretation.

When the issue came to the Security Council in October 2000, the U.S. abstained, apparently not wanting to take such a blatant stand in violation of fundamental principles of international law, particularly given the circumstances of their enactment. The Security Council therefore voted fourteen-zero to call upon Israel to uphold the Convention, which it was again flagrantly violating. Pre-Clinton, the U.S. had voted with the other members to condemn Israel's "flagrant violations" of the Convention. That's consistent with the Clinton practice of effectively rescinding international law and earlier UN decisions for Israel-Palestine.

The media tell us that Arabs believe that the Convention applies to the territories, which is not false, although there's kind of an omission—the Arabs and everybody else. The December 5, 2001, meeting, including all of the European Union, reaffirmed the applicability of the Convention to the territories, the illegality of settlements; called on Israel, meaning the U.S. and Israel, to observe international law. The U.S. boycotted the meeting, thereby killing it. You can check the coverage again.

These acts again contributed to the escalation of terrorism there, including its most severe component, and the media contributed in the usual way.

Responses to Terrorism

Suppose, finally, that we join the Martian observer and we depart from convention radically. We accept moral truisms. If we can rise to that level, we can then, and only then, honestly raise the question of how to respond to terrorist crimes.

One answer is to follow the precedent of law-abiding states, the Nicaraguan precedent, for example. Of course that failed, because they ran up against the fact that the world is ruled by force, not by law, but it wouldn't fail for the U.S. However, evidently that's excluded. I have yet to see one phrase referring to that precedent in the massive coverage of the last couple of months.

Another answer was given by Bush and Boyce, but we instantly reject that one because nobody believes that Haiti or Nicaragua or Cuba and a long list of others around the world have the right to carry out massive terrorist attacks against the United States and its clients, or other rich and powerful states.

A more reasonable answer was given by a number of sources, including the Vatican, and was spelled out by the preeminent Anglo-American military historian, Michael Howard, last October. Actually, it's published in the current issue of *Foreign Affairs* (January-February 2002); that's the leading establishment journal. Now Howard has all the appropriate credentials, a lot of prestige; he's a great admirer of the British Empire, even more extravagantly of its successor in global rule, so he can't be accused of moral relativism or other such crimes.

Referring to September 11, he recommended a police operation against a criminal conspiracy whose members should be hunted down and brought before an international court, where they could receive a fair trial, and if found guilty be awarded an appropriate sentence. That was never contemplated, of course, but it sounds kind of reasonable to me. If it is reasonable, then it ought to hold for even worse terrorist crimes. For example, the U.S. international terrorist attack against Nicaragua, or even worse ones nearby and elsewhere going up to the present. That could never be con-templated, of course, but for opposite reasons.

So honesty leaves us with a dilemma. The easy answer is conventional hypocrisy. The other option is the one adopted by our Martian friend, who actu-ally abides by the principles that we profess with grand self-righteousness. That option is harder to consider, but imperative if the world is to be spared still worse disasters.

ACTS OF AGGRESSION

POLICING "ROGUE STATES"

NOAM CHOMSKY

WITH EDWARD W. SAID

CONTENTS

APOCALYPSE NOW
by Edward W. Said

First published in Arabic in *Al-Hayat*, London,
and in English in *Al Ahram Weekly*, Cairo.

It would be a mistake, I think, to reduce what is happening between Iraq and the United States simply to an assertion of Arab will and sovereignty versus American imperialism, which undoubtedly plays a central role in all this. However misguided, Saddam Hussein's cleverness is not that he is splitting America from its allies (which he has not really succeeded in doing for any practical purpose) but that he is exploiting the astonishing clumsiness and failures of U.S. foreign policy. Very few people, least of all Saddam himself, can be fooled into believing him to be the innocent victim of American bullying; most of what is happening to his unfortunate people who are undergoing the most dreadful and unacknowledged suffering is due in considerable degree to his callous cynicism—first of all, his indefensible and ruinous invasion of Kuwait, his persecution of the Kurds, his cruel egoism and pompous self-regard which persists in aggrandizing himself and his regime at exorbitant and, in my opinion, totally unwarranted cost. It is impossible for him to plead the case for national security and sovereignty given his abysmal disregard of it in the case of Kuwait and Iran. Be that as it may, U.S. vindictiveness, whose sources I shall look at in a moment, has exacerbated the situation by imposing a regime of sanctions which, as Sandy Berger, the American national security adviser has proudly said, is unprecedented for its severity in the whole of world history. It is believed that 567,000 Iraqi civilians have died since the Gulf War, mostly as a result of disease, malnutrition and deplorably poor medical care. Agriculture and industry are at a total standstill. This is unconscionable of course, and for this the brazen inhumanity of American policy-makers is also very largely to blame. But we must not forget that Saddam is feeding that inhumanity quite deliberately in order to dramatize the opposition between the United States and the rest of the Arab world; having provoked a crisis with the United States (or the United Nations dominated by the United States) he at first dramatized the unfairness of the sanctions. But by continuing it, the issue has changed and has become his non-compliance, and the terrible effects of the sanctions have been marginalized. Still the underlying causes of an Arab/U.S. crisis remain. A careful analysis of that crisis is imperative. The United States has always opposed any sign of Arab nationalism or independence, partly for its own imperial reasons and partly because its unconditional support for Israel requires it to do so. Since the 1973 war, and despite the brief oil embargo, Arab policy up to and including the peace process has tried to circumvent or mitigate that hostility by appealing to the United States for help, by "good" behavior, by willingness to make peace with Israel. Yet mere compliance with the wishes of the United States can produce nothing except occasional words of American approbation for leaders who appear "moderate": Arab policy was never backed up with coordination, or collective pressure, or fully agreed upon goals. Instead each leader tried to make separate arrangements both with the United States and with Israel, none of which produced very much except escalating demands and a constant refusal by the United States to exert any meaningful pressure on Israel. The more extreme Israeli policy becomes the more likely the United States has been to support it. And the less respect it has for the large mass of Arab peoples whose future and well-being are mortgaged to illusory hopes embodied, for instance, in the Oslo accords.

Moreover, a deep gulf separates Arab culture and civilization from the United States, and in the absence of any collective Arab information and cultural policy, the notion of an Arab people with traditions, cultures and identities of their own is simply inadmissible in the United States. Arabs are dehumanized, they are seen as violent irrational terrorists always on the lookout for murder and bombing outrages. The only Arabs worth doing business with for the United States are compliant leaders, businessmen, and military people whose arms purchases (the highest per capita in the world) are helping the American economy keep afloat. Beyond that there is no feeling at all, for instance, for the dreadful suffering of the Iraqi people whose identity and existence have simply been lost sight of in the present situation. This morbid, obsessional fear and hatred of the Arabs has been a constant theme in U.S. foreign policy since World War II. In some way also, anything positive about the Arabs is seen in the United States as a threat to Israel. In this respect pro-Israeli American Jews, traditional Orientalists, and military hawks have played a devastating role. Moral opprobrium is heaped on Arab states as it is on no others. Turkey, for example, has been conducting a campaign against the Kurds for several years, yet nothing is heard about this in the United States. Israel occupies territory illegally for thirty years, it violates the Geneva conventions at will, conducts invasions, terrorist attacks and assassinations against Arabs, and still, the United States vetoes every sanction against it in the United Nations. Syria, Sudan, Libya, Iraq are classified as "rogue" states. Sanctions against them are far harsher than against any other countries in the history of U.S.

foreign policy. And still the United States expects that its own foreign policy agenda ought to prevail (e.g., the woefully misguided Doha economic summit) despite its hostility to the collective Arab agenda. In the case of Iraq a number of further extenuations make the United States even more repressive. Burning in the collective American unconscious is a puritanical zeal decreeing the sternest possible attitude towards anyone deemed to be an unregenerate sinner. This clearly guided American policy towards the native American Indians, who were first demonized, then portrayed as wasteful savages, then exterminated, their tiny remnant confined to reservations and concentration camps. This almost religious anger fuels a judgmental attitude that has no place at all in international politics, but for the United States it is a central tenet of its worldwide behavior. Second, punishment is conceived in apocalyptic terms. During the Vietnam war a leading general advocated—and almost achieved—the goal of bombing the enemy into the stone age. The same view prevailed during the Gulf War in 1991. Sinners are meant to be condemned terminally, with the utmost cruelty regardless of whether or not they suffer the cruelest agonies. The notion of "justified" punishment for Iraq is now uppermost in the minds of most American consumers of news, and with that goes an almost orgiastic delight in the power used to confront Iraq in the Gulf.

Pictures of immense U.S. warships steaming virtuously away punctuate breathless news bulletins about Saddam's defiance, and the impending crisis. President Clinton announces that he is thinking not about the Gulf but about the 21st century: how can we tolerate Iraq's threat to use biological warfare even though (this is unmentioned) it is clear from the United Nations Special Committee (UNSCOM) reports that he neither has the missile capacity, nor the chemical arms, nor the nuclear arsenal, nor in fact the anthrax bombs that he is alleged to be brandishing? Forgotten in all this is that the United States has all the terror weapons known to humankind, is the only country to have used a nuclear bomb on civilians, and as recently as seven years ago dropped 66,000 tons of bombs on Iraq. As the only country involved in this crisis that has never had to fight a war on its own soil, it is easy for the United States and its mostly brainwashed citizens to speak in apocalyptic terms. A report out of Australia on Sunday, November 16 suggests that Israel and the United States are thinking about a neutron bomb on Baghdad. Unfortunately the dictates of raw power are very severe and, for a weak state like Iraq, overwhelming. Certainly U.S. misuse of the sanctions to strip Iraq of everything, including any possibility for security is monstrously sadistic. The so-called U.N. 661 Committee created to oversee the sanctions is composed of fifteen member states (including the United States) each of which has a veto. Every time Iraq passes this committee a request to sell oil for medicines, trucks, meat, etc., any member of the committee can block these requests by saying that a given item may have military purposes (tires, for example, or ambulances). In addition, the United States and its clients—e.g., the unpleasant and racist Richard Butler, who says openly that Arabs have a different notion of truth than the rest of the world—have made it clear that even if Iraq is completely reduced militarily to the point where it is no longer a threat to its neighbors (which is now the case) the real goal of the sanctions is to topple Saddam Hussein's government. According to the American government, very little that Iraq can do short of Saddam's resignation or death will produce a lifting of sanctions. Finally, we should not for a moment forget that quite apart from its foreign policy interest, Iraq has now become a domestic American issue whose repercussions on issues unrelated to oil or the Gulf are very important. Bill Clinton's personal crises—the campaign-funding scandals, an impending trial for sexual harassment, his various legislative and domestic failures—require him to look strong, determined and "presidential" somewhere else, and where but in the Gulf against Iraq has he so ready-made a foreign devil to set off his blue-eyed strength to full advantage. Moreover, the increase in military expenditure for new investments in electronic "smart" weaponry, more sophisticated aircraft, mobile forces for the world-wide projection of American power are perfectly suited for display and use in the Gulf, where the likelihood of visible casualties (actually suffering Iraqi civilians) is extremely small, and where the new military technology can be put through its paces most attractively. For reasons that need restating here, the media is particularly happy to go along with the government in bringing home to domestic customers the wonderful excitement of American self-righteousness, the proud flag-waving, the "feel-good" sense that "we" are facing down a monstrous dictator. Far from analysis and calm reflection, the media exists mainly to derive its mission from the government, not to produce a corrective or any dissent. The media, in short, is an extension of the war against Iraq.

The saddest aspect of the whole thing is that Iraqi civilians seem condemned to additional suffering and protracted agony. Neither their government nor that of the United States is inclined to ease the daily pressure on them, and the probability that only they will pay for the crisis is extremely high. At least—and it isn't very much—there seems to be no enthusiasm among Arab governments for American military action, but beyond that there is no coordinated Arab position, not even on the extremely grave humanitarian question. It is unfortunate that, according to the news, there is rising popular support for Saddam in the Arab world, as if the old lessons of defiance without real power have still not been learned. Undoubtedly the United States has manipulated the United Nations to its own ends, a rather shameful exercise given at the same time that the Congress once again struck down a motion to pay a billion dollars in arrears to the world organization. The major priority for Arabs, Europeans, Muslims and Americans is to push to the fore the issue of sanctions and the terrible suffering imposed on innocent Iraqi civilians. Taking the case to the International Court in the Hague strikes me as a perfectly viable possibility, but what is needed is a concerted will on behalf of Arabs who have suffered the U.S.'s egregious blows for too long without an adequate response.

ROGUE STATES

by Noam Chomsky

First published in *Z* magazine, April 1998.

The concept of "rogue state" plays a preeminent role today in policy planning and analysis. The current Iraq crisis is only the latest example. Washington and London declared Iraq a "rogue state," a threat to its neighbors and to the entire world, an "outlaw nation" led by a reincarnation of Hitler who must be contained by the guardians of world order, the United States and its British "junior partner," to adopt the term ruefully employed by the British foreign office half a century ago. The concept merits a closer look. But first, let's consider its application in the current crisis.

The most interesting feature of the debate over the Iraq crisis is that it never took place. True, many words flowed, and there was dispute about how to proceed. But discussion kept within rigid bounds that excluded the obvious answer: the United States and Britain should act in accord with their laws and treaty obligations.

The relevant legal framework is formulated in the Charter of the United Nations, a "solemn treaty" recognized as the foundation of international law and world order, and under the U.S. Constitution, "the supreme law of the land."

The Charter states that "The Security Council shall determine the existence of any threat to the peace, breach of the peace, or act of aggression, and shall make recommendations, or decide what measures shall be taken in accordance with Articles 41 and 42," which detail the preferred "measures not involving the use of armed force" and permit the Security Council to take further action if it finds such measures inadequate. The only exception is Article 51, which permits the "right of individual or collective self-defense" against "armed attack . . . until the Security Council has taken the measures necessary to maintain international peace and security." Apart from these exceptions, member states "shall refrain in their international relations from the threat or use of force."

There are legitimate ways to react to the many threats to world peace. If Iraq's neighbors feel threatened, they can approach the Security Council to authorize appropriate measures to respond to the threat. If the United States and Britain feel threatened, they can do the same. But no state has the authority to make its own determinations on these matters and to act as it chooses; the United States and Britain would have no such authority even if their own hands were clean, hardly the case.

NOAM CHOMSKY

Outlaw states do not accept these conditions: Saddam's Iraq, for example, or the United States. Its position was forthrightly articulated by Secretary of State Madeleine Albright, then U.N. Ambassador, when she informed the Security Council during an earlier U.S. confrontation with Iraq that the United States will act "multilaterally when we can and unilaterally as we must," because "We recognize this area as vital to U.S. national interests" and therefore accept no external constraints. Albright reiterated that stand when U.N. Secretary-General Kofi Annan undertook his February 1998 diplomatic mission: "We wish him well," she stated, "and when he comes back we will see what he has brought and how it fits with our national interest," which will determine how we respond. When Annan announced that an agreement had been reached, Albright repeated the doctrine: "It is possible that he will come with something we don't like, in which case we will pursue our national interest." President Clinton announced that if Iraq fails the test of conformity (as determined by Washington), "everyone would understand that then the United States and hopefully all of our allies would have the unilateral right to respond at a time, place and manner of our own choosing," in the manner of other violent and lawless states.

The Security Council unanimously endorsed Annan's agreement, rejecting U.S./U.K. demands that it authorize their use of force in the event of non-compliance. The resolution warned of "severest consequences," but with no further specification. In the crucial final paragraph, the Council "decides, in accordance with its responsibilities under the Charter, to remain actively seized of the matter, in order to ensure implementation of this resolution and to ensure peace and security in the area." The Council, no one else; in accordance with the Charter.

The facts were clear and unambiguous. Headlines read: "An Automatic Strike Isn't Endorsed" (*Wall Street Journal*); "U.N. Rebuffs U.S. on Threat to Iraq If It Breaks Pact" (*New York Times*); etc. Britain's U.N. Ambassador "privately assured his colleagues on the Council that the resolution does not grant the United States and Britain an 'automatic trigger' to launch strikes against Iraq if it impedes" U.N. searches. "It has to be the Security Council who determines when to use armed force," the Ambassador of Costa Rica declared, expressing the position of the Security Council.

Washington's reaction was different. U.S. Ambassador Bill Richardson asserted that the agreement "did not preclude the unilateral use of force" and that the United States retains its legal right to attack Baghdad at will. State Department spokesperson James Rubin dismissed the wording of the resolution as "not as relevant as the kind of private discussions that we've had": "I am not saying that we don't care about that resolution," but "we've made clear that we don't see the need to return to the Security Council if there is a violation of the agreement." The President stated that the resolution "provides authority to act" if the United States is dissatisfied with Iraq compliance; his press secretary made clear that that means military action. "U.S. Insists It Retains Right to Punish Iraq," the *New York Times* headline read, accurately. The United States has the unilateral right to use force at will: Period.

Some felt that even this stand strayed too close to our solemn obligations under international and domestic law. Senate majority leader Trent Lott denounced the Administration for having "subcontracted" its foreign policy "to others"—to the U.N. Security Council. Senator John McCain warned that "the United States may be subordinating its power to the United Nations," an obligation only for law-abiding states. Senator John Kerry added that it would be "legitimate" for the United States to invade Iraq outright if Saddam "remains obdurate and in violation of the United Nations resolutions, and in a position of threat to the world community," whether the Security Council so determines or not. Such unilateral U.S. action would be "within the framework of international law," as Kerry conceives it. A liberal dove who reached national prominence as an opponent of the

Vietnam War, Kerry explained that his current stand was consistent with his earlier views. Vietnam taught him that the force should be used only if the objective is "achievable and it meets the needs of your country." Saddam's invasion of Kuwait was therefore wrong for only one reason: it was not "achievable," as matters turned out.

At the liberal-dovish end of the spectrum, Annan's agreement was welcomed, but within the narrow framework that barred the central issues. In a typical reaction, the *Boston Globe* stated that had Saddam not backed down, "the United States would not only have been justified in attacking Iraq—it would have been irresponsible not to," with no further questions asked. The editors also called for "a universal consensus of opprobrium" against "weapons of mass destruction" as "the best chance the world has of keeping perverted science from inflicting hitherto unimagined harm." A sensible proposal; one can think of easy ways to start, without the threat of force, but these are not what are intended.

Political analyst William Pfaff deplored Washington's unwillingness to consult "theological or philosophical opinion," the views of Thomas Aquinas and Renaissance theologian Francisco Suarez—as "a part of the analytical community" in the United States and Britain had done "during the 1950s and 1960s," seeking guidance from "philosophy and theology"! But not the foundations of con-

NOAM CHOMSKY

temporary international and domestic law, which are explicit, though irrelevant to the intellectual culture. Another liberal analyst urged the United States to face the fact that if its incomparable power "is really being exercised for mankind's sake, mankind demands some say in its use," which would not be permitted by "the Constitution, the Congress nor television's Sunday pundits"; "And the other nations of the world have not assigned Washington the right to decide when, where and how their interests should be served" (Ronald Steel).

The Constitution does happen to provide such mechanisms, namely, by declaring valid treaties "the supreme law of the land," particularly the most fundamental of them, the U.N. Charter. It further authorizes Congress to "define and punish . . . offenses against the law of nations," undergirded by the Charter in the contemporary era. It is, furthermore, a bit of an understatement to say that other nations "have not assigned Washington the right"; they have forcefully denied it that right, following the (at least rhetorical) lead of Washington, which largely crafted the Charter.

Reference to Iraq's violation of U.N. resolutions was regularly taken to imply that the two warrior states have the right to use force unilaterally, taking the role of "world policemen"—an insult to the police, who in principle are supposed to enforce the law, not tear it to shreds.

There was criticism of Washington's "arrogance of power," and the like, not quite the proper terms for a self-designated violent outlaw state.

One might contrive a tortured legal argument to support U.S./U.K. claims, though no one really tried. Step one would be that Iraq has violated U.N. Resolution 687 of April 3, 1991, which declares a cease-fire "upon official notification by Iraq" that it accepts the provisions that are spelled out (destruction of weapons, inspection, etc.). This is probably the longest and most detailed Security Council Resolution on record, but it mentions no enforcement mechanism. Step two of the argument, then, would be that Iraq's non-compliance "reinvokes" Resolution 678 (November 29, 1990). That Resolution authorizes member states "to use all necessary means to uphold and implement Resolution 660" (August 2, 1990), which calls on Iraq to withdraw at once from Kuwait and for Iraq and Kuwait "to begin immediately intensive negotiations for the resolution of their differences," recommending the framework of the Arab League. Resolution 678 also invokes "all subsequent relevant resolutions" (listing them: 662, 664); these are "relevant" in that they refer to the occupation of Kuwait and Iraqi actions relating to it. Reinvoking 678 thus leaves matters as they were: with no authorization to use force to implement the later Resolution 687, which brings up completely different issues, authorizing nothing beyond sanctions.

There is no need to debate the matter. The United States and Britain could readily have settled all doubts by calling on the Security Council to authorize their "threat and use of force," as required by the Charter. Britain did take some steps in that direction, but abandoned them when it became obvious, at once, that the Security Council would not go along. But these considerations have little relevance in a world dominated by rogue states that reject the rule of law.

Suppose that the Security Council were to authorize the use of force to punish Iraq for violating the cease-fire U.N. Resolution 687. That authorization would apply to all states: for example, to Iran, which would therefore be entitled to invade southern Iraq to sponsor a rebellion. Iran is a neighbor and the victim of U.S.-backed Iraqi aggression and chemical warfare, and could claim, not implausibly, that its invasion would have some local support; the United States and Britain can make no such claim. Such Iranian actions, if imaginable, would never be tolerated, but would be far less outrageous than the plans of the self-appointed enforcers. It is hard to imagine such elementary observations entering public discussion in the United States and Britain.

Contempt for the rule of law is deeply rooted in U.S.

practice and intellectual culture. Recall, for example, the reaction to the judgment of the World Court in 1986 condemning the United States for "unlawful use of force" against Nicaragua, demanding that it desist and pay extensive reparations, and declaring all U.S. aid to the contras, whatever its character, to be "military aid," not "humanitarian aid." The Court was denounced on all sides for having discredited itself. The terms of the judgment were not considered fit to print, and were ignored. The Democrat-controlled Congress immediately authorized new funds to step up the unlawful use of force. Washington vetoed a Security Council resolution calling on all states to respect international law—not mentioning anyone, though the intent was clear.

When the General Assembly passed a similar resolution, the United States voted against it, effectively vetoing it, joined only by Israel and El Salvador; the following year, only the automatic Israeli vote could be garnered. Little of this received mention in the media or journals of opinion, let alone what it signifies.

Secretary of State George Shultz meanwhile explained (April 14, 1986) that "Negotiations are a euphemism for capitulation if the shadow of power is not cast across the bargaining table." He condemned those who advocate "utopian, legalistic means like outside mediation, the United Nations, and the World Court, while ignoring the

NOAM CHOMSKY

power element of the equation"—sentiments not without precedent in modern history.

The open contempt for Article 51 is particularly revealing. It was demonstrated with remarkable clarity immediately after the 1954 Geneva accords on a peaceful settlement for Indochina, regarded as a "disaster" by Washington, which moved at once to undermine them. The National Security Council secretly decreed that even in the case of "local Communist subversion or rebellion *not constituting armed attack*," the United States would consider the use of military force, including an attack on China if it is "determined to be the source" of the "subversion" (NSC 5429/2; my emphasis). The wording, repeated verbatim annually in planning documents, was chosen so as to make explicit the U.S. right to violate Article 51. The same document called for remilitarizing Japan, converting Thailand into "the focal point of U.S. covert and psychological operations in Southeast Asia," undertaking "covert operations on a large and effective scale" throughout Indochina, and in general, acting forcefully to undermine the Accords and the U.N. Charter. This critically important document was grossly falsified by the *Pentagon Papers* historians, and has largely disappeared from history.

The United States proceeded to define "aggression" to include "political warfare, or subversion" (by someone else, that is)—what Adlai Stevenson called "internal aggression" while defending J.F.K.'s escalation to a full-scale attack against South Vietnam. When the United States bombed Libyan cities in 1986, the official justification was "self defense against future attack." *New York Times* legal specialist Anthony Lewis praised the Administration for relying "on a legal argument that violence [in this case] is justified as an act of self-defense," under this creative interpretation of Article 51 of the Charter, which would have embarrassed a literate high school student. The U.S. invasion of Panama was defended in the Security Council by Ambassador Thomas Pickering by appeal to Article 51, which, he declared, "provides for the use of armed force to defend a country, to defend our interests and our people," and entitles the United States to invade Panama to prevent its "territory from being used as a base for smuggling drugs into the United States." Educated opinion nodded sagely in assent.

In June 1993, Clinton ordered a missile attack on Iraq, killing civilians and greatly cheering the president, congressional doves, and the press, who found the attack "appropriate, reasonable and necessary." Commentators were particularly impressed by Ambassador Albright's appeal to Article 51. The bombing, she explained, was in "self-defense against armed attack"—namely, an alleged attempt to assassinate former president Bush two months earlier, an appeal that would have scarcely risen to the level of absurdity even if the United States had been able to demonstrate Iraqi involvement; "Administration officials, speaking anonymously," informed the press "that the judgment of Iraq's guilt was based on circumstantial evidence and analysis rather than ironclad intelligence," the *New York Times* reported, dismissing the matter. The press assured elite opinion that the circumstances "plainly fit" Article 51 (*Washington Post*). "Any President has a duty to use military force to protect the nation's interests" (*New York Times,* while expressing some skepticism about the case in hand). "Diplomatically, this was the proper rationale to invoke," and "Clinton's reference to the U.N. charter conveyed an American desire to respect international law" (*Boston Globe)*. Article 51 "permits states to respond militarily if they are threatened by a hostile power" (*Christian Science Monitor)* Article 51 entitles a state to use force "in self-defence against threats to one's nationals," British Foreign Secretary Douglas Hurd instructed Parliament, supporting Clinton's "justified and proportionate exercise of the right of self-defence." There would be a "dangerous state of paralysis" in the world, Hurd continued, if the United States were required to gain Security Council approval before launching missiles against an enemy that might—or might not—have ordered a failed attempt to kill an ex-President two months earlier.

The record lends considerable support to the concern widely voiced about "rogue states" that are dedicated to the rule of force, acting in the "national interest" as defined by domestic power; most ominously, rogue states that anoint themselves global judge and executioner.

ROGUE STATES: THE NARROW CONSTRUCTION
It is also interesting to review the issues that did enter the non-debate on the Iraq crisis. But first a word about the concept "rogue state."

The basic conception is that although the Cold War is over, the United States still has the responsibility to protect the world—but from what? Plainly it cannot be from the threat of "radical nationalism"—that is, unwillingness to submit to the will of the powerful. Such ideas are only fit for internal planning documents, not the general public. From the early 1980s, it was clear that the conventional technique for mass mobilization was losing its effectiveness: the appeal to J.F.K.'s "monolithic and ruthless conspiracy," Reagan's "evil empire." New enemies were needed.

At home, fear of crime—particularly drugs—was stimulated by "a variety of factors that have little or nothing to do with crime itself," the National Criminal Justice Commission concluded, including media practices and "the role of government and private industry in stoking citizen fear," "exploiting latent racial tension for political purposes," with racial bias in enforcement and sentencing that is devastating black communities, creating a "racial abyss" and putting "the nation at risk of a social catastrophe." The results have been described by criminologists as "the American Gulag," "the new American Apartheid," with African Americans now a majority of prisoners for the first time in U.S. history, imprisoned at well over seven times the rate of whites, completely out of the range of arrest rates, which themselves target blacks far out of proportion to drug use or trafficking.

Abroad, the threats were to be "international terrorism," "Hispanic narcotraffickers," and most serious of all, "rogue states." A secret 1995 study of the Strategic Command, which is responsible for the strategic nuclear arsenal, outlines the basic thinking. Released through the Freedom of Information Act, the study, *Essentials of Post-Cold War Deterrence,* "shows how the United States shifted its deterrent strategy from the defunct Soviet Union to so-called rogue states such as Iraq, Libya, Cuba and North Korea," AP reports. The study advocates that the United States exploit its nuclear arsenal to portray itself as "irrational and vindictive if its vital interests are attacked." That "should be a part of the national persona we project to all adversaries," particularly the "rogue states." "It hurts to portray ourselves as too fully rational and cool-headed," let alone committed to such silliness as international law and treaty obligations. "The fact that some elements" of the U.S. government "may appear to be potentially 'out of control' can be beneficial to creating and reinforcing fears and doubts within the minds of an adversary's decision makers." The report resurrects Nixon's "madman theory": our enemies should recognize that we are crazed and unpredictable, with extraordinary destructive force at our command, so they will bend to our will in fear. The concept was apparently devised in Israel in the 1950s by the governing Labor Party, whose leaders "preached in favor of acts of madness," Prime Minister Moshe Sharett records in his diary, warning that "we will go crazy" ("nishtagea") if crossed, a "secret weapon" aimed in part against the United States, not considered sufficiently reliable at the time. In the hands of the world's sole superpower, which regards itself as an outlaw state and is subject to few constraints from elites within, that stance poses no small problem for the world.

Libya was a favorite choice as "rogue state" from the earliest days of the Reagan administration. Vulnerable and defenseless, it is a perfect punching bag when needed: for example, in 1986, when the first bombing in history orchestrated for prime time TV was used by the Great Communicator's speech writers to muster support for Washington's terrorist forces attacking Nicaragua, on grounds that the "archterrorist" Qaddafi "has sent $400 million and an arsenal of weapons and advisors into Nicaragua to bring his war home to the United States," which was then exercising its right of self-defense against the armed attack of the Nicaraguan rogue state.

Immediately after the Berlin Wall fell, ending any resort to the Soviet threat, the Bush administration submitted its annual call to Congress for a huge Pentagon budget. It explained that "In a new era, we foresee that our military power will remain an essential underpinning of the global balance, but . . . the more likely demands for the use of our military forces may not involve the Soviet Union and may be in the Third World, where new capabilities and approaches may be required," as "when President Reagan directed American naval and air forces to return to [Libya] in 1986" to bombard civilian urban targets, guided by the goal of "contributing to an international environment of peace, freedom and progress within which our democracy—and other free nations—can flourish." The primary threat we face is the "growing technological sophistication" of the Third World. We must therefore strengthen "the defense industrial base"—a.k.a. high tech industry—creating incentives "to invest in new facilities and equipment as well as in research and development." And we must maintain intervention forces, particularly those targeting the Middle East, where the "threats to our interests" that have required direct military engagement "could not be laid at the Kremlin's door"—contrary to endless fabrication, now put to rest. As had occasionally been recognized in earlier years, sometimes in secret, the "threat" is now conceded officially to be indigenous to the region, the "radical nationalism" that has always been a primary concern, not only in the Middle East.

At the time, the "threats to our interests" could not be laid at Iraq's door either. Saddam was then a favored friend and trading partner. His status changed only a few months later, when he misinterpreted U.S. willingness to allow him to modify the border with Kuwait by force as authorization to take the country over—or from the perspective of the Bush administration, to duplicate what the United States had just done in Panama. At a high-level meeting immediately after Saddam's invasion of Kuwait, President Bush articulated the basic problem: "My worry about the Saudis is that they're . . . going to bug out at the last minute and accept a puppet regime in Kuwait." Chair of the Joint Chiefs Colin Powell posed the problem sharply: "The next few days Iraq will withdraw," putting "his puppet in" and "Everyone in the Arab world will be happy."

Historical parallels are never exact, of course. When Washington partially withdrew from Panama after putting its puppet in, there was great anger throughout the hemisphere, including Panama. Indeed throughout much of the world, compelling Washington to veto two Security Council resolutions and to vote against a General Assembly resolution condemning Washington's "flagrant violation of international law and of the independence, sovereignty and territorial integrity of states" and calling for the withdrawal of the "U.S. armed invasion forces from Panama." Iraq's invasion of Kuwait was treated differently, in ways remote from the standard version, but readily discovered in print.

The inexpressible facts shed interesting light on the commentary of political analysts: Ronald Steel, for example, who muses today on the "conundrum" faced by the United States, which, "as the world's most powerful nation, faces greater constraints on its freedom to use force than does any other country." Hence Saddam's success in Kuwait as compared with Washington's inability to exert its will in Panama.

It is worth recalling that debate was effectively foreclosed in 1990-1991 as well. There was much discussion of whether sanctions would work, but none of whether they already had worked, perhaps shortly after Resolution 660 was passed. Fear that sanctions might have worked animated Washington's refusal to test Iraqi withdrawal offers from August 1990 to early January.

With the rarest of exceptions, the information system kept tight discipline on the matter. Polls a few days before the January 1991 bombing showed 2-1 support for a peaceful settlement based on Iraqi withdrawal along with an international conference on the Israel-Arab conflict. Few among those who expressed this position could have heard any public advocacy of it; the media had loyally followed the President's lead, dismissing "linkage" as unthinkable—in this unique case. It is unlikely that any respondents knew that their views were shared by the Iraqi democratic opposition, barred from mainstream media. Or that an Iraqi proposal in the terms they advocated had been released a week earlier by U.S. officials who found it reasonable, and flatly rejected by Washington. Or that an Iraqi withdrawal offer had been considered by the National Security Council as early as mid-August, but dismissed, and effectively suppressed, apparently because it was feared that unmentioned Iraqi initiatives might "defuse the crisis," as the *New York Times* diplomatic correspondent obliquely reported Administration concerns.

Since then, Iraq has displaced Iran and Libya as the leading "rogue state." Others have never entered the ranks. Perhaps the most relevant case is Indonesia, which shifted from enemy to friend when General Suharto took power in 1965, presiding over an enormous slaughter

NOAM CHOMSKY

that elicited great satisfaction in the West. Since then Suharto has been "our kind of guy," as the Clinton administration described him, while carrying out murderous aggression and endless atrocities against his own people; killing 10,000 Indonesians just in the 1980s, according to the personal testimony of "our guy," who wrote that "the corpses were left lying around as a form of shock therapy." In December 1975, the U.N. Security Council unanimously ordered Indonesia to withdraw its invading forces from East Timor "without delay" and called upon "all States to respect the territorial integrity of East Timor as well as the inalienable right of its people to self-determination." The United States responded by (secretly) increasing shipments of arms to the aggressors; Carter accelerated the arms flow once again as the attack reached near-genocidal levels in 1978. In his memoirs, U.N. Ambassador Daniel Patrick Moynihan takes pride in his success in rendering the United Nations "utterly ineffective in whatever measures it undertook," following the instructions of the State Department, which "wished things to turn out as they did and worked to bring this about." The United States also happily accepts the robbery of East Timor's oil (with participation of a U.S. company), in violation of any reasonable interpretation of international agreements.

The analogy to Iraq/Kuwait is close, though there are

differences: to mention only the most obvious, U.S.-sponsored atrocities in East Timor were vastly beyond anything attributed to Saddam Hussein in Kuwait.

There are many other examples, though some of those commonly invoked should be treated with caution, particularly concerning Israel. The civilian toll of Israel's U.S.-backed invasion of Lebanon in 1982 exceeded Saddam's in Kuwait, and it remains in violation of a 1978 Security Council resolution ordering it to withdraw forthwith from Lebanon, along with numerous others regarding Jerusalem, the Golan Heights, and other matters; and there would be far more if the United States did not regularly veto such resolutions. But the common charge that Israel, particularly its current government, is violating U.N. 242 and the Oslo Accords, and that the United States exhibits a "double standard" by tolerating those violations, is dubious at best, based on serious misunderstanding of these agreements. From the outset, the Madrid-Oslo process was designed and implemented by U.S.-Israeli power to impose a Bantustan-style settlement. The Arab world has chosen to delude itself about the matter, as have many others, but they are clear in the actual documents, and particularly in the U.S.-supported projects of the Rabin-Peres governments, including those for which the current Likud government is now being denounced.

It is clearly untrue to claim that "Israel is not demonstrably in violation of Security Council decrees" (*New York Times*), but the reasons often given should be examined carefully.

Returning to Iraq, it surely qualifies as a leading criminal state. Defending the U.S. plan to attack Iraq at a televised public meeting on February 18, Secretaries Albright and Cohen repeatedly invoked the ultimate atrocity: Saddam was guilty of "using weapons of mass destruction against his neighbors as well as his own people," his most awesome crime. "It is very important for us to make clear that the United States and the civilized world cannot deal with somebody who is willing to use those weapons of mass destruction on his own people, not to speak of his neighbors," Albright emphasized in an angry response to a questioner who asked about U.S. support for Suharto. Shortly after, Senator Lott condemned Kofi Annan for seeking to cultivate a "human relationship with a mass murderer," and denounced the Administration for trusting a person who would sink so low.

Ringing words. Putting aside their evasion of the question raised, Albright and Cohen only forgot to mention—and commentators have been kind enough not to point out—that the acts that they now find so horrifying did not turn Iraq into a "rogue state." And Lott failed to note that his heroes Reagan and Bush forged unusually warm relations with the "mass murderer." There were no passionate calls for a military strike after Saddam's gassing of Kurds at Halabja in March 1988; on the contrary, the United States and Britain extended their strong support for the mass murderer, then also "our kind of guy." When ABC TV correspondent Charles Glass revealed the site of one of Saddam's biological warfare programs ten months after Halabja, the State Department denied the facts, and the story died; the Department "now issues briefings on the same site," Glass observes.

The two guardians of global order also expedited Saddam's other atrocities—including his use of cyanide, nerve gas, and other barbarous weapons—with intelligence, technology, and supplies, joining with many others. The Senate Banking Committee reported in 1994 that the U.S. Commerce Department had traced shipments of "biological materials" identical to those later found and destroyed by U.N. inspectors, Bill Blum recalls. These shipments continued at least until November 1989. A month later, Bush authorized new loans for his friend Saddam, to achieve the "goal of increasing U.S. exports and put us in a better position to deal with Iraq regarding its human rights record . . . ," the State Department announced with a straight face, facing no criticism in the mainstream press (or even report).

Britain's record was exposed, at least in part, in an official inquiry (Scott Inquiry). The British government has just now been compelled to concede that it continued to grant licenses to British firms to export materials usable for biological weapons after the Scott report was published, at least until December 1996.

In a February 28 review of Western sales of materials usable for germ warfare and other weapons of mass destruction, the *Times* mentions one example of U.S. sales in the 1980s, including "deadly pathogens," with government approval, some from the Army's center for germ research in Fort Detrick. Just the tip of the iceberg, however.

A common current pretense is Saddam's crimes were unknown, so we are now properly shocked at the discovery and must "make clear" that we civilized folk "cannot deal with" the perpetrator of such crimes (Albright). The posture is cynical fraud. U.N. Reports of 1986 and 1987 condemned Iraq's use of chemical weapons. U.S. Embassy staffers in Turkey interviewed Kurdish survivors of chemical warfare attacks, and the CIA reported them to the State Department. Human Rights groups reported the atrocities at Halabja and elsewhere at once. Secretary of State George Shultz conceded that the United States had evidence on the matter. An investigative team sent by the Senate Foreign Relations Committee in 1988 found "overwhelming evidence of extensive use of chemical weapons against civilians," charging that Western acquiescence in Iraqi use of such weapons against Iran had emboldened Saddam to believe—correctly—that he could use them against his own people with impunity—actually against Kurds, hardly "the people" of this tribal-based thug. The chair of the Committee, Claiborne Pell, introduced the Prevention of Genocide Act of 1988, denouncing silence "while people are gassed" as "complicity," much as when "the world was silent as Hitler began a campaign that culminated in the near extermination of Europe's Jews," and warning that "we cannot be silent to genocide again." The Reagan administration strongly opposed sanctions and insisted that the matter be silenced, while extending its support for the mass murderer. In the Arab world, "the Kuwait press was amongst the most enthusiastic of the Arab media in supporting Baghdad's crusade against the Kurds," journalist Adel Darwish reports.

In January 1991, while the war drums were beating, the International Commission of Jurists observed to the U.N. Human Rights Commission that "After having perpetrated the most flagrant abuses on its own population without a word of reproach from the U.N., Iraq must have concluded it could do whatever it pleased"; United Nations in this context means the United States and

Britain, primarily. That truth must be buried along with international law and other "utopian" distractions.

An unkind commentator might remark that recent U.S./U.K. toleration for poison gas and chemical warfare is not too surprising. The British used chemical weapons in their 1919 intervention in North Russia against the Bolsheviks, with great success according to the British command. As Secretary of State at the War Office in 1919, Winston Churchill was enthusiastic about the prospects of "using poisoned gas against uncivilised tribes"—Kurds and Afghans—and authorized the RAF Middle East command to use chemical weapons "against recalcitrant Arabs as experiment," dismissing objections by the India office as "unreasonable" and deploring the "squeamishness about the use of gas": "we cannot in any circumstances acquiesce in the non-utilisation of any weapons which are available to procure a speedy termination of the disorder which prevails on the frontier," he explained; chemical weapons are merely "the application of Western science to modern warfare."

The Kennedy administration pioneered the massive use of chemical weapons against civilians as it launched its attack against South Vietnam in 1961-1962. There has been much rightful concern about the effects on U.S. soldiers, but not the incomparably worse effects on civilians. In an Israeli mass-circulation daily, the respected journalist Amnon Kapeliouk reported on his 1988 visit to Vietnam, where he found that "Thousands of Vietnamese still die from the effects of American chemical warfare," citing estimates of one-quarter of a million victims in South Vietnam and describing the "terrifying" scenes in hospitals in the south with children dying of cancer and hideous birth deformities. It was South Vietnam that was targeted for chemical warfare, not the North, where these consequences are not found, he reports. There is also substantial evidence of U.S. use of biological weapons against Cuba, reported as minor news in 1977, and at worst only a small component of continuing U.S. terror.

These precedents aside, the United States and Britain are now engaged in a deadly form of biological warfare in Iraq. The destruction of infrastructure and banning of imports to repair it has caused disease, malnutrition, and early death on a huge scale, including 567,000 children by 1995, according to U.N. investigations; UNICEF reports 4,500 children dying a month in 1996. In a bitter condemnation of the sanctions (January 20, 1998), 54 Catholic Bishops quoted the Archbishop of the southern region of Iraq, who reports that "epidemics rage, taking away infants and the sick by the thousands" while "those children who survive disease succumb to malnutrition." The Bishop's statement, reported in full in Stanley

Heller's journal, *The Struggle,* received scant mention in the press. The United States and Britain have taken the lead in blocking aid programs—for example, delaying approval for ambulances on the grounds that they could be used to transport troops, barring insecticides to prevent spread of disease and spare parts for sanitation systems. Meanwhile, western diplomats point out, "The U.S. had directly benefited from [the humanitarian] operation as much, if not more, than the Russians and the French," for example, by purchase of $600 million worth of Iraqi oil (second only to Russia) and sale by U.S. companies of $200 million in humanitarian goods to Iraq. They also report that most of the oil bought by Russian companies ends up in the United States.

Washington's support for Saddam reached such an extreme that it was even willing to overlook an Iraqi air force attack on the USS Stark, killing 37 of the crew, a privilege otherwise enjoyed only by Israel (in the case of the USS Liberty). It was Washington's decisive support for Saddam, well after the crimes that now so shock the Administration and Congress, that led to Iranian capitulation to "Baghdad and Washington," Dilip Hiro concludes in his history of the Iran-Iraq war. The two allies had "co-ordinate[d] their military operations against Teheran." The shooting down of an Iranian civilian airliner by the guided-missile cruiser Vincennes was the culmination of Washington's "diplomatic, military and economic campaign" in support of Saddam, he writes.

Saddam was also called upon to perform the usual services of a client state: for example, to train several hundred Libyans sent to Iraq by the United States so they could overthrow the Qaddafi government, former Reagan White House aide Howard Teicher revealed.

It was not his massive crimes that elevated Saddam to the rank of "Beast of Baghdad." Rather, it was his stepping out of line, much as in the case of the far more minor criminal Noriega, whose major crimes were also committed while he was a U.S. client.

In passing, one might note that the destruction of Iran Air 655 in Iranian airspace by the Vincennes may come back to haunt Washington. The circumstances are suspicious, to say the least. In the Navy's official journal, Commander David Carlson wrote that he "wondered aloud in disbelief" as he observed from his nearby vessel as the Vincennes—then within Iranian territorial waters—shot down what was obviously a civilian airliner in a commercial corridor, perhaps out of "a need to prove the viability of Aegis," its high tech missile system. The commander and key officers "were rewarded with medals for their conduct," Marine Corps colonel (retired) David Evans observes in the same journal in an acid review of the Navy Department cover-up of the affair. President

Bush informed the United Nations that "One thing is clear, and that is that the Vincennes acted in self-defense . . . in the midst of a naval attack initiated by Iranian vessels . . . ," all lies Evans points out, though of no significance, given Bush's position that "I will never apologize for the United States of America—I don't care what the facts are." A retired Army colonel who attended the official hearings concluded that "our Navy is too dangerous to deploy."

It is difficult to avoid the thought that the destruction of Pan Am 103 over Lockerbie a few months later was Iranian retaliation, as stated explicitly by Iranian intelligence defector Abolhassem Mesbahi, also an aide to President Rafsanjani, "regarded as a credible and senior Iranian source in Germany and elsewhere," the *Guardian* reports. A 1991 U.S. intelligence document (National Security Agency), declassified in 1997, draws the same conclusion, alleging that Akbar Mohtashemi, a former Iranian interior minister, transferred $10 million "to bomb Pan Am 103 in retaliation for the U.S. shoot-down of the Iranian Airbus," referring to his connections with "the Al Abas and Abu Nidal terrorist groups." It is striking that despite the evidence and the clear motive, this is virtually the only act of terrorism not blamed on Iran. Rather, the United States and Britain have charged two Libyan nationals with the crime.

The charges against the Libyans have been widely disputed, including a detailed inquiry by Denis Phipps, former head of security at British Airways who served on the government's National Aviation Committee. The British organization of families of Lockerbie victims believe that there has been "a major cover-up" (spokesperson Dr. Jim Swire), and regard as more credible the account given in Alan Frankovich's documentary, *The Maltese Cross,* which provides evidence of the Iranian connection and a drug operation involving a courier working for the U.S. Drug Enforcement Administration. The film was shown at the British House of Commons and on British TV, but rejected here. The U.S. families keep strictly to Washington's version.

Also intriguing is the U.S./U.K. refusal to permit a trial of the accused Libyans. This takes the form of rejection of Libya's offer to release the accused for trial in some neutral venue: to a judge nominated by the U.N. (December 1991), a trial at the Hague "under Scottish law," etc. These proposals have been backed by the Arab League and the British relatives organization but flatly rejected by the United States and Britain. In March 1992, the U.N. Security Council passed a resolution imposing sanctions against Libya, with five abstentions: China, Morocco (the only Arab member), India, Zimbabwe, Cape Verde. There was considerable arm-twisting: thus China was warned

　　　　　　　　　　　　NOAM CHOMSKY

that it would lose U.S. trade preferences if it vetoed the resolution. The U.S. press has reported Libya's offer to release the suspects for trial, dismissing it as worthless and ridiculing Qaddafi's "dramatic gesture" of calling for the surrender of U.S. pilots who bombed two Libyan cities, killing 37 people, including his adopted daughter. Plainly, that is as absurd as requests by Cuba and Costa Rica for extradition of U.S. terrorists.

It is understandable that the United States and Britain should want to ensure a trial they can control, as in the case of the Noriega kidnapping. Any sensible defense lawyer would bring up the Iranian connection in a neutral venue. How long the charade can continue is unclear. In the midst of the current Iraq crisis, the World Court rejected the U.S./U.K. claim that it has no jurisdiction over the matter, and intends to launch a full hearing (13-2, with the U.S. and British judges opposed), which may make it harder to keep the lid on.

The Court ruling was welcomed by Libya and the British families. Washington and the U.S. media warned that the World Court ruling might prejudice the 1992 U.N. resolution that demanded that "Libya must surrender those accused of the Lockerbie bombing for trial in Scotland or the United States" (*New York Times*), that Libya "extradite the suspects to the United States and Britain" (AP). These claims are not accurate. The issue of transfer to Scotland or the United States never arose, and is not mentioned in the U.N. Resolutions. Resolution 731 (January 21, 1992) "Urges the Libyan Government immediately to provide a full and effective response" to requests "in connection with the legal procedures" related to attacks against Pan Am 103 and a French airliner. Resolution 748 (March 31, 1992) "Decides that the Libyan Government must now comply without any further delay" with the request of Resolution 731, and that it renounce terrorism, calling for sanctions if Libya fails to do so. Resolution 731 was adopted in response to a U.S./U.K. declaration that Libya must "surrender for trial all those charged with the crime," with no further specification.

Press reports at the time were similarly inaccurate. Thus, reporting the U.S. dismissal of the Libyan offer to turn the suspects over to a neutral country, the *New York Times* highlighted the words: "Again, Libya tries to avoid a U.N. order." The *Washington Post* dismissed the offer as well, stating that "The Security Council contends that the suspects must be tried in U.S. or British courts." Doubtless Washington prefers to have matters seen in this light. A correct account was given in a 1992 opinion piece by international legal authority Alfred Rubin of the Fletcher School (*Christian Science Monitor*), who noted that the Security Council resolution makes no mention

NOAM CHOMSKY

of extradition to the United States and Britain, and observes that its wording "departs so far from what the United States, Britain, and France are reported to have wanted that current public statements and press accounts reporting an American diplomatic triumph and U.N. pressures on Libya seem incomprehensible"; unfortunately, the performance is all too routine.

In the *New York Times,* British specialist on U.N. law Marc Weiler, in an op-ed, agreed with Rubin that the United States should follow the clear requirements of international law and accept Libya's proposal for World Court adjudication. Libya's response to the U.S./U.K. request was "precisely as mandated by international law," Weiler wrote, condemning the United States and Britain for having "flatly refused" to submit the issue to the World Court. Rubin and Weiler also ask obvious further questions: Suppose that New Zealand had resisted powerful French pressures to compel it to abandon its attempt to extradite the French government terrorists who had bombed the Rainbow Warrior in Auckland harbor? Or that Iran were to demand that the captain of the Vincennes be extradited? The World Court has now drawn the same conclusion as Rubin and Weiler.

The qualifications as "rogue state" are illuminated further by Washington's reaction to the uprisings in Iraq in March 1991, immediately after the cessation of hostilities.

The State Department formally reiterated its refusal to have any dealings with the Iraq democratic opposition, and as from before the Gulf War, they were virtually denied access to the major U.S. media. "Political meetings with them would not be appropriate for our policy at this time," State Department spokesperson Richard Boucher stated. "This time" happened to be March 14, 1991, while Saddam was decimating the southern opposition under the eyes of General Schwartzkopf, refusing even to permit rebelling military officers access to captured Iraqi arms. Had it not been for unexpected public reaction, Washington probably would not have extended even tepid support to rebelling Kurds, subjected to the same treatment shortly after.

Iraqi opposition leaders got the message. Leith Kubba, head of the London-based Iraqi Democratic Reform Movement, alleged that the United States favors a military dictatorship, insisting that "changes in the regime must come from within, from people already in power." London-based banker Ahmed Chalabi, head of the Iraqi National Congress, said that "the United States, covered by the fig leaf of non-interference in Iraqi affairs, is waiting for Saddam to butcher the insurgents in the hope that he can be overthrown later by a suitable officer," an attitude rooted in the U.S. policy of "supporting dictatorships to maintain stability."

NOAM CHOMSKY

Administration reasoning was outlined by *New York Times* chief diplomatic correspondent Thomas Friedman. While opposing a popular rebellion, Washington did hope that a military coup might remove Saddam, "and then Washington would have the best of all worlds: an iron-fisted Iraqi junta without Saddam Hussein," a return to the days when Saddam's "iron fist . . . held Iraq together, much to the satisfaction of the American allies Turkey and Saudi Arabia," not to speak of Washington. Two years later, in another useful recognition of reality, he observed that "it has always been American policy that the iron-fisted Mr. Hussein plays a useful role in holding Iraq together," maintaining "stability." There is little reason to believe that Washington has modified the preference for dictatorship over democracy deplored by the ignored Iraqi democratic opposition, though it doubtless would prefer a different "iron fist" at this point. If not, Saddam will have to do.

The concept "rogue state" is highly nuanced. Thus Cuba qualifies as a leading "rogue state" because of its alleged involvement in international terrorism, but the United States does not fall into the category despite its terrorist attacks against Cuba for close to 40 years, apparently continuing through last summer according to important investigative reporting of the *Miami Herald,* which failed to reach the national press (in the United

States; it did in Europe). Cuba was a "rogue state" when its military forces were in Angola, backing the government against South African attacks supported by the United States. South Africa, in contrast, was not a rogue state then, nor during the Reagan years, when it caused over $60 billion in damage and 1.5 million deaths in neighboring states according to a U.N. commission, not to speak of some events at home—and with ample U.S./U.K. support. The same exemption applies to Indonesia and many others.

The criteria are fairly clear: a "rogue state" is not simply a criminal state, but one that defies the orders of the powerful—who are, of course, exempt.

MORE ON "THE DEBATE"

That Saddam is a criminal is undoubtedly true, and one should be pleased, I suppose, that the United States and Britain, and mainstream doctrinal institutions, have at last joined those who "prematurely" condemned U.S./U.K. support for the mass murderer. It is also true that he poses a threat to anyone within his reach. On the comparison of the threat with others, there is little unanimity outside the United States and Britain, after their (ambiguous) transformation from August 1990. Their 1998 plan to use force was justified in terms of Saddam's threat to the region, but there was no way to conceal the

NOAM CHOMSKY

fact that the people of the region objected to their salvation, so strenuously that governments were compelled to join in opposition.

Bahrein refused to allow U.S./British forces to use bases there. The president of the United Arab Emirates described U.S. threats of military action as "bad and loathsome," and declared that Iraq does not pose a threat to its neighbors. Saudi Defense Minister Prince Sultan had already stated that "We'll not agree and we are against striking Iraq as a people and as a nation," causing Washington to refrain from a request to use Saudi bases. After Annan's mission, long-serving Saudi foreign minister Prince Saud al-Faisal reaffirmed that any use of Saudi air bases "has to be a U.N., not a U.S. issue."

An editorial in Egypt's quasi-official journal, *Al Ahram,* described Washington's stand as "coercive, aggressive, unwise and uncaring about the lives of Iraqis, who are unnecessarily subjected to sanctions and humiliation," and denounced the planned U.S. "aggression against Iraq." Jordan's Parliament condemned "any aggression against Iraq's territory and any harm that might come to the Iraqi people"; the Jordanian army was forced to seal off the city of Maan after two days of pro-Iraq rioting. A political science professor at Kuwait University warned that "Saddam has come to represent the voice of the voiceless in the Arab world," expressing popular frustration over the "New World Order" and Washington's advocacy of Israeli interests.

Even in Kuwait, support for the U.S. stance was at best "tepid" and "cynical over U.S. motives," the press recognized. "Voices in the streets of the Arab world, from Cairo's teeming slums to the Arabian Peninsula's shiny capitals, have been rising in anger as the American drumbeat of war against Iraq grows louder," *Boston Globe* correspondent Charles Sennott reported.

The Iraqi democratic opposition was granted a slight exposure in the mainstream, breaking the previous pattern. In a telephone interview with the *New York Times,* Ahmed Chalabi reiterated the position that had been reported in greater detail in London weeks earlier: "Without a political plan to remove Saddam's regime, military strikes will be counter-productive," he argued, killing thousands of Iraqis, leaving Saddam perhaps even strengthened along with his weapons of mass destruction and with "an excuse to throw out UNSCOM [the U.N. inspectors]," who have in fact destroyed vastly more weapons and production facilities than the 1991 bombing. U.S./U.K. plans would "be worse than nothing." Interviews with opposition leaders from several groups found "near unanimity" in opposing military action that did not lay the basis for an uprising to overthrow Saddam. Speaking to a Parliamentary committee, Chalabi held that it was "morally indefensible to strike Iraq without a strategy" for removing Saddam.

In London, the opposition also outlined an alternative program: (1) declare Saddam a war criminal; (2) recognize a provisional Iraqi government formed by the opposition; (3) unfreeze hundreds of millions of dollars of Iraqi assets abroad; restrict Saddam's forces by a "no-drive zone" or extend the "no-flight zone" to cover the whole country. The United States should "help the Iraqi people remove Saddam from power," Chalabi told the Senate Armed Services Committee. Along with other opposition leaders, he "rejected assassination, covert U.S. operations or U.S. ground troops," Reuters reported, calling instead for "a popular insurgency." Similar proposals have occasionally appeared in the United States. Washington claims to have attempted support for opposition groups, but their own interpretation is different. Chalabi's view, published in England, is much as it was years earlier; "everyone says Saddam is boxed in, but it is the Americans and British who are boxed in by their refusal to support the idea of political change."

Regional opposition was regarded as a problem to be evaded, not a factor to be taken into account, any more than international law. The same was true of warnings by senior U.N. and other international relief officials in Iraq that the planned bombing might have a "catastrophic" effect on people already suffering miserably, and might terminate the humanitarian operations that have brought at least some relief. What matters is to establish that "What We Say Goes," as President Bush triumphantly proclaimed, announcing the New World Order as bombs and missiles were falling in 1991.

As Kofi Annan was preparing to go to Baghdad, former Iranian president Rafsanjani, "still a pivotal figure in Tehran, was given an audience by the ailing King Fahd in Saudi Arabia," British Middle East correspondent David Gardner reported, "in contrast to the treatment experienced by Madeleine Albright . . . on her recent trips to Riyadh seeking support from America's main Gulf ally." As Rafsanjani's ten-day visit ended on March 2, foreign minister Prince Saud described it as "one more step in the right direction towards improving relations," reiterating that "the greatest destabilising element in the Middle East and the cause of all other problems in the region" is Israel's policy towards the Palestinians and U.S. support for it, which might activate popular forces that Saudi Arabia greatly fears, as well as undermining its legitimacy as "guardian" of Islamic holy places, including the Dome of the Rock in East Jerusalem, now effectively annexed by U.S./Israeli programs as part of their intent to extend "greater Jerusalem" virtually to the Jordan Valley, to be retained by Israel. Shortly before, the Arab states had boycotted a U.S.-sponsored economic summit in Qatar that was intended to advance the "New Middle East" project of Clinton and Peres. Instead, they attended an Islamic conference in Teheran in December, joined even by Iraq.

These are tendencies of considerable import, relating to the background concerns that motivate U.S. policy in the region: its insistence, since World War II, on controlling the world's major energy reserves. As many have observed, in the Arab world there is growing fear and resentment of the long-standing Israel-Turkey alliance that was formalized in 1996, now greatly strengthened. For some years, it had been a component of the U.S. strategy of controlling the region with "local cops on the beat," as Nixon's Defense Secretary put the matter. There is apparently a growing appreciation of the Iranian advocacy of regional security arrangements to replace U.S. domination. A related matter is the intensifying conflict over pipelines to bring Central Asian oil to the rich countries, one natural outlet being via Iran.

And U.S. energy corporations will not be happy to see foreign rivals—now including China and Russia as well—gain privileged access to Iraqi oil reserves, second only to Saudi Arabia in scale, or to Iran's natural gas, oil, and other resources.

For the present, Clinton planners may well be relieved

to have escaped temporarily from the "box" they had constructed that was leaving them no option but a bombing of Iraq that could have been harmful even to the interests they represent. The respite is temporary. It offers opportunities to citizens of the warrior states to bring about changes of consciousness and commitment that could make a great difference in the not too distant future.

APPENDIX

ON THE FIFTIETH ANNIVERSARY OF THE UNIVERSAL DECLARATION OF HUMAN RIGHTS

by Ramsey Clark

"The world has never had a good definition of the word liberty, and the American people, just now, are much in want of one. We all declare for liberty, but in using the same word we do not all mean the same thing." So observed Abraham Lincoln at, for him, the darkest moment of the American Civil War. He had just received reports of the massacre of 800 Union soldiers, former slaves whose ancestors were brought from Africa in chains. They were the first such unit to be engaged in combat. Caught and overwhelmed at Ft. Pillow, Tennessee, on the Mississippi River by a much larger Confederate cavalry force under Nathan Bedford Forrest, every man was killed. Forrest reported the river ran red for hundreds of yards. After the war Forrest was a founder of the Ku Klux Klan and engaged in racist violence for two decades.

Four score and four years after the Ft. Pillow massacre, in the Preamble to the Universal Declaration of Human Rights on December 10, 1948, the U.N. General Assembly found "a common understanding of these rights and freedoms is of the greatest importance," and proclaimed its declaration in order to provide "a good definition."

The Universal Declaration was dominated by the experience, concerns, interests and values of a narrow segment of the "people of the United Nations," primarily the governments of the rich nations, primarily the United States, England and France. It emphasized political rights developed over centuries from their histories with little concern for economic, social and cultural rights. Still it was and remains an important contribution in the continuing struggle for justice.

In the fifth paragraph of its preamble the Declaration notes the United Nations has affirmed ". . . the dignity and worth of the human person and the equal rights of men and women and have determined to promote social progress and better standards of life in larger freedom." Article 1 provides "All human beings are born free and equal in dignity and rights." Article 5 states "No one shall be subjected to torture or to cruel, inhuman or degrading treatment or punishment." Article 25 declares "(1) Everyone has the right to a standard of living adequate for the health and well-being of himself and of his family, including food, clothing, housing and medical care . . ."

The United States government pays lip service to the Declaration, but its courts have consistently refused to enforce its provisions reasoning it is not a legally binding treaty, or contract, but only a declaration. This ignores the fact that international law recognizes the provisions of the Declaration as being incorporated into customary international law which is binding on all nations.

The most fundamental, dangerous and harmful violation of the Universal Declaration of Human Rights on its fifteenth birthday is economic sanctions imposed on entire populations. The United States alone blockades eleven million Cubans in the face of the most recent General Assembly resolution approved by 157 nations condemning the blockade, with only the United States and Israel in opposition. The entire population of Cuba and every Cuban has had the "right to a standard of living adequate for health and well-being . . . including food, clothing, housing and medical care" deliberately violated by the United States blockade.

Security Council sanctions against Iraq, which are forced by the United States, have devastated the entire nation, taking the lives of more than 1,500,000 people, mostly infants, children, chronically ill and elderly, and harming millions more by hunger, sickness and sorrow. The sanctions destroy the "dignity and rights" of the people of Iraq and are the most extreme form of "cruel, inhuman and degrading treatment," which are prohibited by the Declaration.

Despite the cruelest destruction of the most basic human rights and liberties of all the people in Iraq, including rights to medicine, safe drinking water and sufficient food, the United States government, with the major mass media in near perfect harmony, proclaims itself the world's champion of liberty and human rights. The problem as Lincoln surely knew is not merely one of definitions. It is a problem of power, will and accountability. The United States intends to have its way and serve its own interests, with Iraq, Cuba, Libya, Iran, the Sudan and many other countries whatever the consequences to the liberties and rights of those who live there.

The United States control over and its concerted action with the mass media enables it to demonize such countries, its victims, for "terrorism," threats to world peace and human rights violations at the very time it rains Tomahawk cruise missiles on them and motivates and finances armed insurrections and violence against them. At the same time the United States increases its own staggeringly large prison industry, with more than a million persons confined, including 40 percent of all African-American males between 17 and 27 years old in the State of California. Simultaneously the United States spends more on its military than the ten largest military budgets of other nations combined, sells most of the arms and sophisticated weapons still increasing world-

　　　　　　　　　　　　RAMSEY CLARK

wide while rejecting an international convention to prohibit land mines and an international court of criminal justice. And the United States maintains and deploys the great majority of all weapons of mass destruction existent on earth, nuclear, chemical, biological and the most deadly of all—economic sanctions.

It is imperative that clear definitions of all fundamental rights of people, be clearly inscribed in international law, including economic rights which are most basic to human need and on which all other rights are dependent and rights to freedom from military aggression by a superpower or its surrogates.

But without a passionate commitment by the people of the United States and other major powers to stop their own governments from violating those definitions of human rights, hold them accountable for their acts and to prevent their own media from seducing them into acceptance or complacency, there will be no protection for the poor and powerless and no correspondence between the words of rich and powerful nations and their deeds.

We can be thankful for the Universal Declaration of Human Rights, but together the people of the world must do better to define and protect the humanity of the people.

EDWARD W. SAID was born in Jerusalem, Palestine, and attended schools there and in Cairo, Egypt. He is Old Dominion Foundation Professor in the Humanities at Columbia University. He is the author of *Orientalism, Covering Islam, After the Last Sky, Culture and Imperialism,* and many others. He was formerly a member of the Palestine National Council

RAMSEY CLARK is an attorney, teacher, and writer. He served as Attorney General of the United States during the Johnson Administration. He is actively engaged in practice of law in fields of law, peace, disarmament, human rights, civil rights, civil liberties, voting rights, health, education and others. In 1991 he founded the International Action Center.

ABOUT THE AUTHOR

NOAM CHOMSKY is a world renowned political activist, writer, and professor of linguistics at Massachusetts Institute of Technology, where he has taught since 1955. Chomsky has written and lectured widely on linguistics, philosophy, and politics. His most recent book is the international bestseller *9-11*. Among his other works are: *Powers and Prospects; World Orders, Old and New; Deterring Democracy; Manufacturing Consent* (with E. S. Herman); *Year 501: The Conquest Continues; Profit Over People;* The *New Military Humanism; New Horizons in the Study of Language and Mind; Rogue States;* and *A New Generation Draws the Line.* Chomsky's efforts for greater democracy are celebrated by peace and social justice movements worldwide.

ABOUT SEVEN STORIES PRESS

SEVEN STORIES PRESS is an independent book publisher based in New York City, with distribution throughout the United States, Canada, England, and Australia. We publish works of the imagination by such writers as Nelson Algren, Octavia E. Butler, Assia Djebar, Ariel Dorfman, Lee Stringer, and Kurt Vonnegut, to name a few, together with political titles by voices of conscience, including the Boston Women's Health Book Collective, Noam Chomsky, Ralph Nader, Gary Null, Project Censored, Barbara Seaman, Gary Webb, and Howard Zinn, among many others. Our books appear in hardcover, paperback, pamphlet, and e-book formats, in English and in Spanish. We believe publishers have a special responsibility to defend free speech and human rights wherever we can.

For more information about us, visit our Web site at www.sevenstories.com or write for a free catalogue to Seven Stories Press, 140 Watts Street, New York, NY 10013.

ABOUT OPEN MEDIA PAMPHLETS AND BOOKS

OPEN MEDIA is a movement-oriented publishing project committed to the vision of "one world in which many worlds fit"— a world with social justice, democracy, and human rights for all people. Founded during wartime in 1991, Open Media has a ten year history of producing critically acclaimed and best-selling books and pamphlets that address our most urgent political and social issues.

Before and after September 11, Open Media has produced an array of anti-war works that focus on terrorism, "rogue states," U.S. propaganda, militarism, and the implications of U.S. foreign and domestic policies on human rights and civil liberties. These titles include:

9-11 by Noam Chomsky

Acts of Aggression: Policing "Rogue" States by Noam Chomsky with Edward W. Said

Bin Laden, Islam, and America's New "War on Terrorism" by As`ad AbuKhalil

Islands of Resistance: Puerto Rico, Vieques, and U.S. Policy by Mario Murillo

Israel/Palestine: How to End the War of 1948 by Tanya Reinhart

Media Control: The Spectacular Achievements of Propaganda by Noam Chomsky

Propaganda, Inc. by Nancy Snow

Secret Trials and Executions by Barbara Olshansky

Sent by Earth by Alice Walker

Silencing Political Dissent by Nancy Chang

Terrorism: Theirs and Ours by Eqbal Ahmad

Terrorism and War by Howard Zinn

The Umbrella of U.S. Power by Noam Chomsky

Weapons in Space by Karl Grossman

Visit the Seven Stories Press web site for updated information and a complete list of all available Open Media books and pamphlets.

openmedia@sevenstories.com | www.sevenstories.com